SUNK AT SEA

R. M. BALLANTYNE

1st WORLD
LIBRARY
Literary Society

Sunk at Sea

R. M. Ballantyne

© 1st World Library, 2009
PO Box 2211
Fairfield, IA 52556
www.1stworldlibrary.com
First Edition

LCCN: 2009923491

Softcover ISBN: 978-1-4218-8876-7
Hardcover ISBN: 978-1-4218-8975-7
eBook ISBN: 978-1-4218-8777-7

Purchase *"Sunk at Sea"*
as a traditional bound book at:
www.1stWorldLibrary.com/purchase.asp?ISBN=978-1-4218-8876-7

1st World Library is a literary, educational organization
dedicated to:

- Creating a free internet library of downloadable ebooks

- Hosting writing competitions and offering book
  publishing scholarships.

1st World Library Literary Society

Giving Back to the World

"If you want to work on the core problem, it's early school literacy."

- James Barksdale, former CEO of Netscape

"No skill is more crucial to the future of a child, or to a democratic and prosperous society, than literacy."

- Los Angeles Times

"Literacy... means far more than learning how to read and write... The aim is to transmit... knowledge and promote social participation."

- UNESCO

"Literacy is not a luxury, it is a right and a responsibility. If our world is to meet the challenges of the twenty-first century we must harness the energy and creativity of all our citizens."

- President Bill Clinton

"Parents should be encouraged to read to their children, and teachers should be equipped with all available techniques for teaching literacy, so the varying needs and capacities of individual kids can be taken into account."

- Hugh Mackay

CHAPTER ONE

TREATS OF OUR HERO'S EARLY LIFE, AND TOUCHES ON DOMESTIC MATTERS

William Osten was a wanderer by nature. He was born with a thirst for adventure that nothing could quench, and with a desire to rove that nothing could subdue.

Even in babyhood, when his limbs were fat and feeble, and his visage was round and red, he displayed his tendency to wander in ways and under circumstances that other babies never dreamt of. He kept his poor mother in a chronic fever of alarm, and all but broke the heart of his nurse, long before he could walk, by making his escape from the nursery over and over again, on his hands and knees; which latter bore constant marks of being compelled to do the duty of feet in dirty places.

Baby Will never cried. To have heard him yell would have rejoiced the hearts of mother and nurse, for that would have assured them of his being near at hand and out of mischief—at least not engaged in more than ordinary mischief. But Baby Will was a natural philosopher from his birth. He displayed his wisdom by holding his peace at all times, except when very hard pressed by hunger or pain, and appeared to regard life in general in a grave, earnest, inquiring spirit. Nevertheless, we would not have it understood that Will was a slow, phlegmatic baby. By no means. His silence was deep, his gravity profound, and his earnestness intense, so that, as a rule, his existence was unobtrusive. But his energy was tremendous. What he undertook to do he usually did with all his might and main—whether it was the rending of his pinafore or the smashing of his drum!

We have said that he seldom or never cried, but he sometimes laughed, and that not unfrequently; and when he did so you could not choose but hear, for his whole soul gushed out in his laugh, which was rich, racy, and riotous. He usually lay down and rolled when he laughed, being quite incapable of standing to do it—at least during the early period of babyhood. But Will would not laugh at everything. You could not make him laugh by cooing and smirking and talking nonsense, and otherwise making an ass of yourself before him.

Maryann, the nurse, had long tried that in vain, and had almost broken her heart about it. She was always breaking her heart, more or less, about her charge, yet, strange to say, she survived that dreadful operation, and ultimately lived to an extreme old age!

"Only think," she was wont to say to Jemima Scrubbins, her bosom friend, the monthly nurse who had attended Will's mother, and whose body was so stiff, thin, and angular, that some of her most intimate friends thought and said she must have been born in her skeleton alone— "Only think, Jemimar, I give it as my morial opinion that that hinfant 'asn't larfed once—no, not once—durin' the last three days, although I've chirruped an' smiled an' made the most smudgin' faces to it, an' heaped all sorts o' blandishments upon it till—. Oh! you can't imagine; but

R. M. Ballantyne

nothink's of any use trying of w'en you can't do it; as my 'usband, as was in the mutton-pie line, said to the doctor the night afore he died—my 'art is quite broken about it, so it is."

To which Jemima was wont to reply, with much earnestness—for she was a sympathetic soul, though stiff, thin, and angular—"You don't say so, Maryhann! P'raps it's pains."

Whereupon Maryann would deny that pains had anything to do with it, and Jemima would opine that it was, "koorious, to say the least of it."

No, as we have said, Baby Will would not laugh at everything. He required to see something really worth laughing at before he would give way, and when he did give way, his eyes invariably disappeared, for his face was too fat to admit of eyes and mouth being open at the same time. This was fortunate, for it prevented him for a little from seeing the object that tickled his fancy, and so gave him time to breathe and recruit for another burst. Had it been otherwise, he would certainly have suffocated himself in infancy, and this, his veracious biography, would have remained unwritten!

To creep about the house into dangerous and forbidden places, at the risk of life and limb, was our hero's chief delight in early childhood. To fall out of his cradle and crib, to tumble down stairs, and to bruise his little body until it was black and blue, were among his most ordinary experiences. Such mishaps never drew tears, however, from his large blue eyes. After struggling violently to get over the rail of his crib, and falling heavily on the floor, he was wont to rise with a gasp, and gaze in bewilderment straight before him, as if he were rediscovering the law of gravitation. No phrenologist ever conceived half the number of bumps that were developed on his luckless cranium.

We make no apology to the reader for entering thus minutely into the character and experiences of a baby. That baby is the hero of our tale. True, it is as a young man that he is to play his part; but a great philosopher has told us that he always felt constrained to look upon children with respect; and a proverb states that, "the child is the father of the man."

Without either pinning our faith to the philosopher or the proverb, we think it both appropriate and interesting to note the budding genius of the wanderer whose footsteps we are about to follow.

Baby Will's mother was a gentle and loving, but weak woman. His father, William Horace Osten by name, was a large, hearty, affectionate, but coarse man. He appreciated his wife's gentle, loving nature, but could not understand her weakness. She admired her husband's manly, energetic spirit, but could not understand his roughness. He loved the baby, and resolved to "make a man of him." She loved the baby, and wished to make him a "good boy." In the furtherance of their designs the one tried to make him a lion, the other sought to convert him into a lamb. Which of the two would have succeeded can never be known. It is probable that both would have failed by counteracting each other, as is no uncommon experience when fathers and mothers act separately in such a matter. If the one had succeeded, he would have made him a bear. The other, if successful, would have made him a nincompoop. Fortunately for our hero, a higher power saved him, and, by training him in the school of adversity, made him both a lion and a lamb. The training was very severe and

R. M. Ballantyne

prolonged, however.

It was long before the lion would consent to lie down in the same breast with the lamb. Certainly it was not during the season of childhood. The lion appeared to have it all his own way during that interesting epoch, and the father was proportionately gratified, while the mother was dismayed.

Boyhood came, and with it an increased desire to rove, and a more fervent thirst for adventure. At school our hero obtained the name that stuck to him through life— "Wandering Will." The seaport town in the west of England in which he dwelt had been explored by him in all its ramifications. There was not a retired court, a dark lane, or a blind alley, with which he was unfamiliar. Every height, crag, cliff, plantation, and moor within ten miles of his father's mansion had been thoroughly explored by Will before he was eight years of age, and his aspiring spirit longed to take a wider flight.

"I want to go to sea, father," said he one evening after tea, looking in his father's face with much more of the leonine gaze than the father had bargained for. His training up to that point had been almost too successful!

This was not the first time that the boy had stated the same wish; his gaze, therefore, did not quail when his father looked up from his newspaper and said sternly— "Fiddlesticks, boy! hold your tongue."

"Father," repeated Will, in a tone that caused Mr Osten to lay down his paper, "I want to go to sea."

"Then the sooner you give up the idea the better, for I won't let you."

"Father," continued Will, "you remember the proverb that you've often told me has been your motto through life, 'Never venture never win?'"

"Certainly; you know that I have often urged you to act on that principle at school. Why do you ask the question?"

"Because I mean to act on it now, and go to sea," replied Will firmly.

"What? without permission, without clothes, and without money; for you shan't have a six-pence from me?"

"Yes," replied Will.

Mr Osten was one of those stern, despotic men who cannot bear to be thwarted. He was a rich merchant, and almost the king of the little town in which he dwelt. His greatest ambition was to make his only son a thorough man of business. To be spoken to in such a tone by that rebellious son was too much for him. He lost his temper, leaped up, and, seizing Will by the collar, thrust him out of the room.

The boy ran to his own bedroom, and, seating himself in front of the dressing-table, hit that piece of furniture with his clenched fist so violently that all its contents leaped up and rattled.

"Dear, dear Will," said a gentle voice at his side, while a loving hand fell on his shoulder, "why do you frown so fiercely?"

"How can I help it, mother, when he treats me like that? He is harsh and unfair to me."

R. M. Ballantyne

"Not so unfair as you think, dear Will," said his mother.

We will not detail the arguments by which the good lady sought to combat her son's desires. Suffice it to say that she succeeded—as only mothers know how—in lulling the lion to sleep at that time, and in awakening the lamb. Wandering Will went back to school with a good grace, and gave up all idea of going to sea.

CHAPTER TWO

RECORDS A SUDDEN DEPARTURE, AND MARYANN'S OPINION THEREON

There is a fallacy into which men and women of mature years are apt to fall—namely, that the cares and sorrows of the young are light.

How many fathers and mothers there are who reason thus —"Oh, the child will grow out of this folly. 'Tis a mere whim—a youthful fancy, not worthy of respect,"— forgetting or shutting their eyes to the fact, that, light though the whim or fancy may be in their eyes, it has positive weight to those who cherish it, and the thwarting of it is as destructive of peace and joy to the young as the heavier disappointments of life are to themselves.

True, the cares and sorrows of the young are light in the sense that they are not usually permanent. Time generally blows them away, while the cares of later years often remain with us to the end. But they are not the less real, heavy, and momentous at the time on that account.

Those troubles cannot with propriety be called light which drive so many young men and women to rebellion and to destruction. Well would it have been for Mr Osten if he had treated his son like a rational being, instead of calling him a "young fool," and commanding him to "obey."

Will, however, was not an untractable young lion. He went through school and entered college, despite his unconquerable desire to go to sea, in obedience to his father's wishes. Then he resolved to study medicine. Mr Osten regarded the time thus spent as lost, inasmuch as his son might have been better employed in learning "the business" to which he was destined; still he had no great objection to his son taking the degree of MD, so he offered no opposition; but when Will, at the age of eighteen, spoke to him of his intention to take a run to the north or south seas, as surgeon in a whaler, he broke out on him.

"So, it seems that your ridiculous old fancy still sticks to you," said Mr Osten, in great wrath, for the recurrence of the subject was like the lacerating of an old sore.

"Yes, father; it has never left me. If you will listen for a few moments to my reasons—"

"No, boy," interrupted his father, "I will *not* listen to your reasons. I have heard them often enough—too often—and they are foolish, false, utterly inconclusive. You may go to Jericho as far as I am concerned; but if you do go, you shall never darken my doors again."

"When I was a boy, father," said Will earnestly, "your speaking sharply to me was natural, for I was foolish, and acted on impulse. I am thankful now that I did not give way to rebellion, as I was tempted to do; but I am not now a boy, father. If you will talk calmly with me—"

"Calmly!" interrupted Mr Osten, growing still more angry

at the quiet demeanour of his son; "do you mean to insinuate that—that—. What do you mean, sir?"

"I insinuate nothing, father; I mean that I wish you to hear me patiently."

"I *won't* hear you," cried Mr Osten, rising from his chair, "I've heard you till I'm tired of it. Go if you choose, if you dare. You know the result."

Saying this he left the room hastily, shutting the door behind him with a bang.

A grave, stern expression settled on the youth's countenance as he arose and followed him into the passage. Meeting his mother there, he seized her suddenly in his arms and held her in a long embrace; then, without explaining the cause of his strong emotion, he ran down stairs and left his father's house.

In a dirty narrow street, near the harbour of the town, there stood a small public-house which was frequented chiefly by the sailors who chanced to be in the port, and by the squalid population in its immediate neighbourhood. Although small, the Red Lion Inn was superior in many respects to its surroundings. It was larger than the decayed buildings that propped it; cleaner than the locality that owned it; brighter and warmer than the homes of the lean crew on whom it fattened. It was a pretty, light, cheery, snug place of temptation, where men and women, and even children assembled at nights to waste their hard-earned cash and ruin their health. It was a place where the devil reigned, and where the work of murdering souls was carried on continually,—nevertheless it was a "jolly" place. Many good songs were sung there, as well as bad ones; and many a rough grasp of hearty friendship was exchanged. Few people, going into the house for a few minutes, could have brought themselves to believe that it was such a *very* broad part of the road leading to destruction: but the landlord had some hazy notion on that point. He sat there day and night, and saw the destruction going on. He saw the blear-eyed, fuddled men that came to drown conscience in his stalls, and the slatternly women who came and went. Nevertheless he was a rosy, jocund fellow who appeared to have a good deal of the milk of human kindness about him, and would have looked on you with great surprise, if not scorn, had you told him that he had a hand in murdering souls. Yes! the Red Lion might have been appropriately styled the Roaring Lion, for it drove a roaring trade among the poor in that dirty little street near the harbour.

The gas was flaring with attractive brilliancy in the Red Lion when Will Osten entered it, and asked if Captain Dall was within.

"No, sir," answered the landlord; "he won't be here for half-an-hour yet."

"A pot of beer," said Will, entering one of the stalls, and sitting down opposite a tall, dark-countenanced man, who sat smoking moodily in a corner.

It was evident that our hero had not gone there to drink, for the beer remained untouched at his elbow, as he sat with his face buried in his hands.

The dark man in the corner eyed him steadily through the smoke which issued from his lips, but Will paid no attention to him. He was too deeply absorbed in his own reflections.

"A fine night, stranger," he said at length, in a slightly nasal tone.

Still Will remained absorbed, and it was not until the remark had been twice repeated that he looked up with a start.

"I beg pardon; did you speak?" he said. "Well, yes," drawled the dark man, puffing a long white cloud from his lips, "I did make an observation regardin' the weather. It looks fine, don't it?"

"It does," said Will.

"You're waitin' for Captain Dall, ain't you?"

"Why, how did *you* come to know that?" said Will.

"I didn't come to know it, I guessed it," said the dark man.

At that moment the door opened, and a short thick-set man, in a glazed hat and pea-jacket, with huge whiskers meeting under his chin, entered.

His eye at once fell upon the dark man, whom he saluted familiarly—"All ready, Mr Cupples?"

"All ready, sir," replied the other; "it's now more than half-flood; in three hours we can drop down the river with the first of the ebb, and if this breeze holds we'll be in blue water before noon to-morrow."

"Hallo, doctor, is that yourself?" said the captain, whose eye had for some moments rested on Will.

"It is," said the youth, extending his hand, which the other

R. M. Ballantyne

grasped and shook warmly.

"What! changed your mind—eh?"

"Yes, I'm going with you."

"The governor bein' agreeable?" inquired the captain.

Will shook his head.

"Hope there ain't bin a flare-up?" said the captain earnestly.

"Not exactly," said Will; "but he is displeased, and will not give his consent, so I have come away without it."

At this the jovial skipper, who was styled captain by courtesy, sat down and shook his head gravely, while he removed his hat and wiped the perspiration from his bald forehead.

"It's a bad business to run agin the wishes of one's parents," he said; "it seldom turns out well; couldn't you come round him nohow?"

"Impossible. He won't listen to reason."

"Ah, then, it's of no manner of use," said the captain, with a pitying sigh, "when a man won't listen to reason, what's the consequence? why he's unreasonable, which means bein' destitoot of that which raises him above the brutes that perish. Such bein' the case, give it up for a bad job, that's my advice. Come, I'll have a bottle o' ginger-beer, not bein' given to strong drink, an' we'll talk over this matter."

Accordingly the beer was ordered, and the three sat there talking for a couple of hours in reference to a long, long voyage to the southern seas.

After that they rose, and, leaving the Red Lion, went down to the pier, where a boat was in waiting. It conveyed them to a large ship, whose sails were hanging in the loose condition peculiar to a vessel ready to set sail. An hour after that the anchor was raised, and wind and tide carried the ship gently down to the sea. There seemed to Will something very solemn and mysterious in the quiet way in which, during these still and dark hours of the night, the great ship was slowly moved towards her ocean cradle. At length she floated on the sea, and, soon after, the moon arose on the distant horizon, streaming across the rippling surface as if to kiss and welcome an old friend. The wind increased; the ship became submissive to the breeze, obedient to the helm, and ere long moved on the waters like "a thing of life," leaving Old England far behind her.

It was then that young Osten, leaning over the taffrail and looking wistfully back at the point where he had seen the last glimpse of the chalk cliffs, began to experience the first feelings of regret. He tried to quiet his conscience by recalling the harsh and unjustifiable conduct of his father, but conscience would not be quieted thus, and faithful memory reminded him of the many acts of kindness he had experienced at his father's hands, while she pointed to his gentle mother, and bade him reflect what a tremendous blow this sudden departure would be to her.

Starting up and shaking off such thoughts, sternly he went below and threw himself into his narrow cot, where conscience assailed him still more powerfully and vividly in dreams. Thus did Wandering Will leave his native land.

R. M. Ballantyne

Commenting on his sudden departure, two days afterwards, Maryann said, in strict confidence, to her bosom friend "Jemimar," that she "know'd it would 'appen—or somethink simular, for, even w'en a hinfant, he had refused to larf at her most smudgin' blandishments; and that she knew somethink strange would come of it, though she would willingly have given her last shilling to have prevented it, but nothink was of any use tryin' of w'en one couldn't do it, as her 'usband, as was in the mutton-pie line, said to the doctor the night afore he died,—and that her 'art was quite broken about it, so it was."

Whereupon Jemima finished to the dregs her last cup of tea, and burst into a flood of tears.

CHAPTER THREE

TELLS OF THE SEA, AND SOME OF THE MYSTERIES CONNECTED THEREWITH

For many days and nights the good ship *Foam* sailed the wide ocean without encountering anything more than the ordinary vicissitudes and experiences of sea-life. Dolphins were seen and captured, sharks were fished for and caught, stiff breezes and calms succeeded each other, constellations in the far north began to disappear and new constellations arose in the southern skies. In fact, during many weeks the voyage was prosperous, and young Will Osten began to experience those peculiar feelings with which all travellers are more or less acquainted—he felt that the ship was "home"; that his cabin with its furniture, which had appeared so small and confined at first, was quite a large and roomy place; that all the things about him were positive realities, and that the home of his childhood was a shadow of the past—a sort of dream.

During all this time the young doctor led a busy life. He was one of those active, intelligent, inquiring spirits which cannot rest. To acquire information was with him not a duty, but a pleasure. Before he had been many days at sea he knew the name and use of every rope, sail, block, tackle, and spar in the ship, and made himself quite

R. M. Ballantyne

a favourite with the men by the earnestness with which he questioned them in regard to nautical matters and their own personal experiences. George Goff, the sail-maker, said he "was a fust-rate feller;" and Larry O'Hale, the cook, declared, "he was a trump intirely, an' ought to have been born an Irishman." Moreover, the affections of long Mr Cupples (as the first mate was styled by the men) were quite won by the way in which he laboured to understand the use of the sextant, and other matters connected with the mysteries of navigation; and stout Jonathan Dall, the captain, was overjoyed when he discovered that he was a good player on the violin, of which instrument he was passionately fond. In short, Will Osten became a general favourite on board the *Foam*, and the regard of all, from the cabin-boy to the captain, deepened into respect when they found that, although only an advanced student and, "not quite a doctor," he treated their few ailments with success, and acted his part with much self-possession, gentleness, and precision.

Larry O'Hale was particularly eloquent in his praises of him ever after the drawing of a tooth which had been the source of much annoyance to the worthy cook. "Why, messmates," he was wont to say, "it bait everything the way he tuk it out. 'Open yer mouth,' says he, an' sure I opened it, an' before I cud wink, off wint my head—so I thought—but faix it wor only my tuth—a real grinder wi' three fangs no less—och! he's a cliver lad intirely."

But Will did not confine his inquiries to the objects contained within his wooden home. The various phases and phenomena of the weather, the aspects of the sky, and the wonders of the deep, claimed his earnest attention. To know the reason of everything was with him a species of mania, and in pursuit of this knowledge he stuck at nothing. "Never venture never win," became with him as favourite a motto as it had been with his father, and he acted on it more vigorously than his father had ever done.

One calm evening, as he was leaning over the side of the ship near the bow, gazing contemplatively down into the unfathomable sea, he overheard a conversation between the cook and one of the sailors named Muggins. They were smoking their pipes seated on the heel of the bowsprit.

"Larry," said Muggins, "I think we have got into the doldrums."

"Ye're out there, boy," said Larry, "for I heerd the capting say we wos past 'em a long way."

The men relapsed into silence for a time.

Then Muggins removed his pipe and said—

"Wot ever caused the doldrums?"

"That's more nor I can tell," said Larry; "all I know about them is, that it's aisy to git into them, but uncommon hard to git out again. If my ould grandmother was here, she'd be able to tell us, I make no doubt, but she's in Erin, poor thing, 'mong the pigs and the taties."

"Wot could *she* tell about the doldrums?" said Muggins, with a look of contempt.

"More nor ye think, boy; sure there isn't nothin' in the univarse but she can spaik about, just like a book, an' though she niver was in the doldrums as far as I knows, she's been in the dumps often enough; maybe it's cousins they are. Anyhow she's not here, an' so we must be contint

R. M. Ballantyne

with spekilation."

"What's that you say, Larry?" inquired the captain, who walked towards the bow at the moment.

The cook explained his difficulty.

"Why, there's no mystery about the doldrums," said Captain Dall. "I've read a book by an officer in the United States navy which explains it all, and the Gulf Stream, and the currents, an' everything. Come, I'll spin you a yarn about it."

Saying this, the captain filled and lighted his pipe, and seating himself on the shank of the anchor, said—

"You know the cause of ocean currents, I dare say?"

"Niver a taste," said Larry. "It's meself is as innocent about 'em as the babe unborn; an' as for Muggins there, *he* don't know more about 'em than my ould shoes—"

"Or your old grandmother," growled Muggins.

"Don't be irriverent, ye spalpeen," said Larry.

"I ax her reverence's pardon, but I didn't know she wos a priest," said Muggins.—"Go on, Cap'n Dall."

"Well," continued the captain, "you know, at all events, that there's salt in the sea, and I may tell you that there is lime also, besides other things. At the equator, the heat bein' great, water is evaporated faster than anywhere else, so that there the sea is salter and has more lime in it than elsewhere. Besides that it is hotter. Of course, that being the case, its weight is different from the waters of the cold polar seas, so it is bound to move away an' get itself freshened and cooled. In like manner, the cold water round the poles feels obliged to flow to the equator to get itself salted and warmed. This state of things, as a natural consequence, causes commotion in the sea. The commotion is moreover increased by the millions of shell-fish that dwell there. These creatures, not satisfied with their natural skins, must needs have shells on their backs, and they extract lime from the sea-water for the purpose of makin' these shells. This process is called secretin' the lime; coral insects do the same, and, as many of the islands of the south seas are made by coral insects, you may guess that a considerable lot of lime is made away with. The commotion or disturbance thus created produces two great currents—from the equator to the poles and from the poles to the equator. But there are many little odds and ends about the world that affect and modify these currents, such as depth, and local heat and cold, and rivers and icebergs, but the chief modifiers are continents. The currents flowin' north from the Indian Ocean and southern seas rush up between Africa and America. The space bein' narrow—comparatively—they form one strong current, on doublin' the Cape of Good Hope, which flies right across to the Gulf of Mexico. Here it is turned aside and flows in a nor'-easterly direction, across the Atlantic towards England and Norway, under the name of the Gulf Stream, but the Gulf of Mexico has no more to do with it than the man in the moon, 'xcept in the way of turnin' it out of its nat'ral course. This Gulf Stream is a *river of warm water* flowing through the cold waters of the Atlantic; it keeps separate, and wherever it flows the climate is softened. It embraces Ireland, and makes the climate there so mild that there is, as you know, scarcely any frost all the year round—"

"Blissin's on it," broke in Larry, " sure that accounts for

the purty green face of Erin, which bates all other lands in the world. Good luck to the Gulf Stream, say I!"

"You're right, Larry, and England, Scotland, and Norway have reason to bless it too, for the same latitudes with these places in America have a rigorous winter extendin' over more than half the year. But what I was comin' to was this—there are, as you know, eddies and stagnant places in ornary rivers, where sticks, leaves, and other odds and ends collect and remain fixed. So, in this great ocean river, there are eddies where seaweed collects and stagnates, and where the air above also stagnates (for the air currents are very much like those of the sea). These eddies or stagnant parts are called sargasso seas. There are several of them, of various sizes, all over the ocean, but there is one big one in the Atlantic, which is known by the name of the 'Doldrums.' It has bothered navigators in all ages. Columbus got into it on his way to America, and hundreds of ships have been becalmed for weeks in it since the days of that great discoverer. It is not very long since it was found out that, by keeping well out of their way, and sailing round 'em, navigators could escape the Doldrums altogether."

The captain paused at this point, and Larry O'Hale took the opportunity to break in.

"D'ye know, sir," said he, "that same Gulf Strame has rose a lot o' pecooliar spekilations in my mind, which, if I may make so bowld, I'll—"

Here the mate's voice interrupted him gruffly with—

"Shake out a reef in that top-gall'n s'l; look alive, lads!"

Larry and his comrades sprang to obey. When they

returned to their former place in the bow, the captain had left it, so that the cook's "pecooliar spekilations" were not at that time made known.

R. M. Ballantyne

CHAPTER FOUR

A STORM AND ITS CONSEQUENCES

In course of time the *Foam*, proceeding prosperously on her voyage, reached the region of Cape Horn—the cape of storms. Here, in days of old, Magellan and the early voyagers were fiercely buffeted by winds and waves. In later days Cook and others met with the same reception. In fact, the Cape is infamous for its inhospitality, nevertheless it shone with bright smiles when the *Foam* passed by, and a gentle fair-wind wafted her into the great Pacific Ocean. Never, since that eventful day when the adventurous Castilian, Vasco Nunez de Balboa, discovered this mighty sea, did the Pacific look more peaceful than it did during the first week in which the *Foam* floated on its calm breast. But the calm was deceitful. It resembled the quiet of the tiger while crouching to make a fatal spring.

Will Osten reclined against the top of the mainmast, to which he had ascended in order to enjoy, undisturbed, the quiet of a magnificent evening.

The sun was setting in a world of clouds, which took the form of mountains fringed with glittering gold and with shadows of pearly grey.

Oh what castles young Osten did build on these mountains, to be sure! Structures so magnificent that Eastern architects, had they seen them, would have hung their heads and confessed themselves outdone. But you must not imagine, reader, that the magnificence of all of these depended on their magnitude or richness. On the contrary, one of them was a mere cottage—but then, it was a pattern cottage. It stood in a palm-wood, on a coral island near the sea-shore, with a stream trickling at its side, and a lake full of wild fowl behind, and the most gorgeous tropical plants clustering round its open windows and door, while inside, seated on a couch, was a beautiful girl of fifteen (whom Will had often imagined, but had not yet seen), whose auburn hair shone like gold in the sun, contrasting well with her lovely complexion, and enhancing the sweetness of a smile which conveyed to the beholder only one idea—love. Many other castles were built in the clouds at that time by Will, but the cottage made the most lasting impression on his mind.

"Sleepin'?" inquired Cupples, the mate, thrusting his head through that orifice in the main-top which is technically called the "lubber's hole."

"No, meditating," answered Will; "I've been thinking of the coral islands."

"Humph," ejaculated the mate contemptuously, for Cupples, although a kind-hearted man, was somewhat cynical and had not a particle of sentiment in his soul. Indeed he showed so little of this that Larry was wont to say he "didn't belave he had a sowl at all, but was only a koorious specimen of an animated body."

"It's my opinion, doctor, that you'd as well come down, for it's goin' to blow hard."

Will looked in the direction in which the mate pointed, and saw a bank of black clouds rising on the horizon. At the same moment the captain's voice was heard below shouting—"Stand by there to reef topsails!" This was followed by the command to close-reef. Then, as the squall drew rapidly nearer, a hurried order was giving to take in all sail. The squall was evidently a worse one than had at first been expected.

On it came, hissing and curling up the sea before it.

"Mind your helm!—port a little, port!"

"Port it is, sir," answered the man at the wheel, in the deep quiet voice of a well-disciplined sailor, whose only concern is to do his duty.

"Steady!" cried the captain.

The words had barely left his lips, and the men who had been furling the sails had just gained the deck, when the squall struck them, and the *Foam* was laid on her beam-ends, hurling all her crew into the scuppers. At the same time terrible darkness overspread the sky like a pall. When the men regained their footing, some of them stood bewildered, not knowing what to do; others, whose presence of mind never deserted them, sprang to where the axes were kept, in order to be ready to cut away the masts if necessary. But the order was not given.

Captain Dall and Will, who had been standing near the binnacle, seized and clung to the wheel.

"She will right herself," said the former, as he observed that the masts rose a little out of the sea.

Fortunately the good ship did so, and then, although there was scarcely a rag of canvas upon her, she sprang away before the hurricane like a sea-gull.

Terrible indeed is the situation of those who are compelled to "scud under bare poles," when He who formed the great deep, puts forth His mighty power, causing them to "stagger and be at their wits' end." For hours the *Foam* rushed wildly over the sea, now rising like a cork on the crest of the billows, anon sinking like lead into the valleys between. She was exposed to double danger; that of being cast upon one of the numerous coral reefs with which the Pacific in some parts abounds, or being "pooped" and overwhelmed by the seas which followed her.

During this anxious period little was said or done except in reference to the working of the ship. Men snatched sleep and food at intervals as they best might. At length, after two days, the gale began to abate, and the sea to go down.

"It was sharp while it lasted, captain, but it seems to have done us little harm," said Will Osten, on the evening of the second day.

"True," said the captain heartily; "we'll soon repair damages and make all snug.—Is there much water in the hold, Mr Cupples?"

The mate answered gloomily that there was a good deal.

It must not be supposed that Mr Cupples' gloominess arose from anxiety. Not at all. It was simply his nature to be gloomy. If it had been his duty to have proclaimed the approach of his own marriage, he would have done it as

R. M. Ballantyne

sadly as if it had been the announcement of his death. His thoughts were gloomy, and his tones were appropriate thereto. Even his jokes were grave, and his countenance was lugubrious.

"It is gaining on us, sir," added Mr Cupples.

"Then get all the spare hands to work with buckets immediately," said the captain, "and send the carpenter here; we must have the leak discovered."

"Yes, sir," sighed Mr Cupples, as if he had given way to despair; nevertheless, he went off actively to obey the order.

"A strange man that," said the captain, turning to Will; "he is a capital seaman, and a kind-hearted, honest fellow, yet he is melancholy enough to throw a man into the blues."

"He and I get on famously notwithstanding," said Will, with a laugh. "See, he is running aft—with bad news I fear, for his face is longer if possible than—"

"Leak's increasing, sir," said the mate hurriedly; "we must have started a plank."

This seemed to be too true. All hands were now plying pumps and buckets vigorously, and every effort was being made to discover the leak, but in vain. Hour by hour, inch by inch, the water gained on them, and it soon became apparent that the ship must sink.

It is difficult for those who have never been at sea to realise the feelings of men who are thus suddenly awakened to the awful fact that the vessel which has been their home for many weeks or months can no longer be counted on, and that, in a few hours, they shall be left in open boats, far from land, at the mercy of the wide and stormy sea. So terrible was the thought to those on board the *Foam*, that every man, from the captain to the cabin-boy, toiled for hours at the pumps in silent desperation. At last, when it was found that the water gained on them rapidly, and that there was no hope of saving the ship, the captain quietly left off working and put on his coat.

"Avast pumping, my lads," said he, in a grave, earnest tone; the good ship is doomed, and now it behoves us to bow to the will of the Lord, and do the best we can to save our lives. Stand by to hoist out the boats. Get up bread and water, steward, and stow in them as much as you can with safety. Mr Cupples, see my orders carried out, and have the provisions properly divided among the boats. I want you, doctor, to come below, and help me to get up a few things that will be of use to us.

The prompt energy of the captain infused confidence into the men, who soon executed the orders given them. Ere long the boats were ready to be launched over the side, but this was a matter of the greatest difficulty and danger, for the sea was still running high, and the ship rolled heavily.

And now the great evil of not being provided with proper tackling to launch the boats became apparent. One of the quarter-boats was the first to be lowered; it was full of men. The order was given to lower, and it dropped on the water all right. Then the order to unhook the tackle was given. The man at the stern tackle succeeded in unhooking, but the man at the bow failed. The result was fatal and instantaneous. When the ship rose on the next wave, the boat was lifted by the bow out of the water until

R. M. Ballantyne

she hung from the davits, and a terrible cry was uttered as all the men were thrown out of her into the sea. Next moment the boat was plunged into the waves, the tackle snapt, and she was swept away.

"Lower away the long-boat!" shouted the captain.

This was eagerly and quickly done, and the mate with a number of men leaped into it. The lowering was successfully accomplished, but when they pulled to the spot where the quarter-boat had gone down, not one of those who had manned her could be found. All had perished.

The remaining four boats were lowered in safety, and all of them pulled away from the sinking ship, for latterly she had been settling down so deep that it was feared every pitch would be her last, and had she sunk while the boats were alongside, their destruction would have been inevitable. They were rowed, therefore, to a safe distance, and there awaited the end.

There was something inexpressibly sad in this. It seemed like standing at the death-bed of an old friend. The sea was still heaving violently; the gale, although moderated, was still pretty stiff, and the sun was setting in wild lurid clouds when the *Foam* rose for the last time—every spar and rope standing out sharply against the sky. Then she bent forward slowly, as she overtopped a huge billow. Into the hollow she rushed. Like an expert diver she went down head foremost into the deep, and, next moment, those who had so lately trod her deck saw nothing around them save the lowering sky and the angry waters of the Pacific Ocean.

CHAPTER FIVE

ADRIFT ON THE WIDE OCEAN

For some time after the disappearance of the ship, the men in the boats continued to gaze, in a species of unbelief, at the place where she had gone down. They evidently felt it difficult to realise the truth of what they had seen. The suddenness of the change and the extreme danger of their position might have shaken the stoutest hearts, for the sea still ran high and none of the boats were fitted to live in rough weather. They were, as far as could be judged, many hundreds of miles from land, and, to add to the horror of their circumstances, night was coming on.

"My lads," said Captain Dall, sitting down in the stern of his boat, and grasping the tiller, "it has pleased the Almighty to sink our ship and to spare our lives. Let us be thankful that we didn't go to the bottom along with her. To the best of my knowledge we're a long way from land, and all of us will have to take in a reef in our appetites for some time to come. I have taken care to have a good supply of salt junk, biscuit, water, and lime-juice put aboard, so that if the weather don't turn out uncommon bad, we may manage, with God's blessing, to make the land. In circumstances of this kind, men's endurance is sometimes tried pretty sharply, and men in distress are

R. M. Ballantyne

occasionally driven to forgetting their duty to their comrades. I tell you beforehand, lads, that I will do all that in me lies to steer you to the nearest port, and to make your lot as comfortable as may be in an open boat; but if any of you should take a fancy to having his own way, I've brought with me a little leaden pill-box (here the captain drew aside the breast of his coat and exposed the handle of a revolver) which will tend to keep up discipline and prevent discord. Now, lads, ship your oars and hoist the foresail close-reefed, and look alive, for it seems to me that we'll have a squally night."

The effect of this speech was very striking. There is nothing that men dislike so much, in critical circumstances, where action is necessary, as uncertainty or want of decision on the part of their leader. The loss of their ship, and their forlorn, almost desperate condition, had sunk their spirits so much that an air of apathetic recklessness had, for a few minutes, crossed the countenances of some of the boldest among the sailors; but while the captain was speaking this expression passed away, and when he had finished they all gave one hearty cheer, and obeyed his orders with alacrity.

In a few minutes the sails, closely reefed, were hoisted, and the long-boat rushed swiftly over the waves. At first the four boats kept company—the other three having also made sail—but as darkness set in they lost sight of each other. The first mate had charge of the jolly-boat, and the second mate and carpenter had the two others. In the captain's boat were Will Osten, Larry O'Hale, Goff, Muggins, and several of the best seamen.

Soon after the sails were set, a heavy sea broke inboard and nearly filled the boat.

"Bail her out, lads," shouted the captain.

There was no occasion for the order, the men knew their danger well enough, and every one seized anything that came to hand and began to bail for life. There was only one bucket on board, and this was appropriated by the cook, who, being one of the strongest men in the boat, thought himself entitled to the post of honour, and, truly, the way in which Larry handled that bucket and showered the water over the side justified his opinion of himself.

"We must rig up something to prevent that happening again," said Captain Dall; "set to work, Goff, and cut a slice out of the tarpaulin, and nail it over the bows."

This was done without delay, and in less than an hour a sort of half-deck was made, which turned off the spray and rendered the task of bailing much lighter—a matter of considerable importance, for, in such a sea, there was no possibility of an open boat remaining afloat without constant bailing.

At first the men talked a good deal in comparatively cheerful tones while they worked, and the irrepressible Larry O'Hale even ventured to cut one or two jokes; but when night began to cover the deep with thick darkness, one after another dropped out of the conversation, and at last all were perfectly silent, except when it became necessary to give an order or answer a question, and nothing was heard save the whistling of the wind and the gurgling of the waves as they rushed past, their white crests curling over the edge of the boat as if greedy to swallow her, and gleaming like lambent fire all around.

"This is a terrible situation," said Will Osten, in a low tone, with an involuntary shudder. "Do you think there is

R. M. Ballantyne

much chance of our surviving, captain?"

"That's not an easy question to answer, doctor," replied Captain Dall, in a tone so hearty that our hero was much cheered by it. "You see, there is much in our favour as well as much against us. In the first place, this is the Pacific, and according to its name we have a right to expect more fine weather than bad, especially at this time of the year. Then we have the trade winds to help us, and our boat is a good one, with at least two weeks' provisions aboard. But then, on the other hand, we're a terrible long way off land, and we must count upon a gale now and then, which an open boat, however good, is not calc'lated to weather easily. See that now," added the captain, looking back over the stern, where, from out of the darkness, Osten could just see a huge wave, like a black mountain with a snowy top, rolling towards them. "If we were only a little more down in the stern, that fellow would drop on board of us and send us to the bottom in half a minute."

Will felt that, although the captain's tones were reassuring, his words were startling. He was ill at ease, and clutched the seat when the billow rolled under them, raising the stern of the boat so high that it seemed as if about to be thrown completely over, but the wave passed on, and they fell back into the trough of the sea.

"Musha! but that was a wathery mountain no less," exclaimed Larry.

"You've heard of Captain Bligh, Larry, I suppose?" said the captain, in a loud voice, with the intention of letting the men hear his remarks.

"May be I have," replied Larry with caution, "but if so

I misremimber."

"He was the captain of the *Bounty*, whose crew mutinied and turned him adrift in an open boat in the middle of the Pacific. What I was goin' to tell ye was, that his circumstances were a trifle worse than ours, for he was full four thousand miles from the nearest land, and with short allowance of provisions on board."

"An' did he make out the voyage, sur?" asked Larry.

"He did, and did it nobly too, in the face of great trouble and danger, but it's too long a yarn to spin just now; some day when the weather's fine I'll spin it to 'ee. He weathered some heavy gales, too, and what one man has done another man may do; so we've no reason to get down-hearted, for we're nearer land than he was, and better off in every way. I wish I could say as much for the other boats."

The captain's voice dropped a little in spite of himself as he concluded, for, despite the strength and buoyancy of his spirit, he could not help feeling deep anxiety as to the fate of his companions in misfortune.

Thus, talking at intervals in hopeful tones, and relapsing into long periods of silence, they spent that stormy night without refreshment and without rest. The minutes seemed to float on leaden wings, and the weary watchers experienced in its highest degree that dreary feeling—so common in the sick room—that "morning would *never* come."

But morning came at length—a faint glimmer on the eastern horizon. It was hailed by Larry with a deep sigh, and the earnest exclamation—

"Ah, then, there's the blessed sun at last, good luck to it!"

Gradually the glimmer increased into grey dawn, then a warm tint brightened up the sky, and golden clouds appeared. At last the glorious sun arose in all its splendour, sending rays of warmth to the exhausted frames of the seamen and hope to their hearts. They much needed both, for want of sleep, anxiety, and cold, had already stamped a haggard look of suffering on their faces. As the morning advanced, however, this passed away, and by degrees they began to cheer up and bestir themselves,—spreading out their clothes to dry, and scanning the horizon at intervals in search of the other boats.

About eight o'clock, as nearly as he could guess, the captain said—

"Now, lads, let's have breakfast; get out the bread-can. Come, Larry, look alive! You've no cooking to do this morning, but I doubt not that your teeth are as sharp and your twist as strong as ever."

"Stronger than iver, sur, av ye plaze."

"I'm sorry to hear it, for you'll have to go on short allowance, I fear."

"Ochone!" groaned the cook.

"Never mind, Larry," said Will Osten, assisting to spread the sea-biscuit and salt junk on one of the thwarts; "there's a good time coming."

"Sure, so's Christmas, doctor, but it's a long way off," said Larry.

"Fetch me the scales; now then, doctor, hold 'em," said the captain, carefully weighing out a portion of biscuit and meat which he handed to one of the men. This process was continued until all had been supplied, after which a small quantity of water and lime-juice was also measured out to each.

The breakfast was meagre, but it was much needed, and as the sea had gone down during the night and the morning was beautiful, it was eaten not only in comfort, but with some degree of cheerfulness. While they were thus engaged, Goff looked up and exclaimed suddenly, "Hallo! look here, boys!"

Every one started up and gazed in the direction indicated, where they saw something black floating on the water. The captain, who had taken the precaution before leaving the ship to sling his telescope over his shoulder, applied it to his eye, and in a few seconds exclaimed, "It's the jolly-boat capsized! Out with the oars, boys—be smart! There's some of 'em clinging to the keel."

It need scarcely be said that the men seized the oars and plied them with all their might. Under the influence of these and the sail together they soon drew near, and then it was distinctly seen that three men were clinging to the boat—it followed, of course, that all the rest must have been drowned. Silently and swiftly they pulled alongside, and in a few minutes had rescued Mr Cupples and the steward and one of the sailors, all of whom were so much exhausted that they could not speak for some time after being taken on board. When they could tell what had happened, their tale was brief and sad. They had kept in sight of the long-boat while light enabled them to do so. After that they had run before the gale, until a heavy sea capsized them, from which time they could remember

R. M. Ballantyne

nothing, except that they had managed to get on the bottom of the upturned boat, to which they had clung for many hours in a state of partial insensibility.

CHAPTER SIX

DESCRIBES A BOAT VOYAGE,
AND TOUCHES ON CORAL ISLANDS

The gale moderated to a fresh breeze, and all that day the long-boat of the ill-fated *Foam* flew over the sea towards the west.

"You see," said Captain Dall, in answer to a question put to him by Will Osten, "I don't know exactly whereabouts we are, because there was a longish spell of dirty weather afore the *Foam* went down, and I hadn't got a sight o' the sun for more than a week; but it's my belief that we are nearer to some of the coral islands than to the coast of South America, though how near I cannot tell. Five hundred miles, more or less, perhaps."

"A mere trifle, sure!" said Larry, filling his pipe carefully —for his was the only pipe that had been rescued from the sinking ship, and the supply of tobacco was very small. Small as it was, however, the captain had taken the precaution to collect it all together, causing every man to empty his pockets of every inch that he possessed, and doled it out in small equal quantities. The pipe, however, could not be treated thus, so it had to be passed round— each man possessing it in turn for a stated number of

R. M. Ballantyne

minutes, when, if he had not consumed his portion, he was obliged to empty the pipe and give it up.

"It's my turn, Larry," cried Muggins, holding out his hand for the coveted implement of fumigation.

"No, ye spalpeen, it's not," said Larry, continuing to press down the precious weed, "owld Bob had it last, an' ivery wan knows that I come after him."

"It's the first time I ever heard ye admit that you comed after anybody," answered Muggins with a grin; "ye ginerally go before us all—at least ye want to."

"Not at all," retorted the cook; "whin there's dirty work to be done, I most usually kape modestly in the background, an' lets you go first, bekase it's your nat'ral callin'. Arrah! the sun's goin' to set, boys," he added with a sigh, as he commenced to smoke.

This was true, and the knowledge that another long night of darkness was about to set in depressed the spirits which had begun to revive a little. Silence gradually ensued as they sat watching the waves or gazing wistfully towards the gorgeous mass of clouds in which the sun was setting. For a considerable time they sat thus, when suddenly Will Osten started up, and, pointing towards the horizon a little to the left of the sun, exclaimed—

"Look there, captain; what's that?"

"Land ho!" shouted Larry O'Hale at that moment, springing up on the thwart and holding on to the foremast.

All the rest leaped up in great excitement.

"It's only a cloud," said one.

"It's a fog-bank," cried another.

"I never seed a fog-bank with an edge like that," observed old Bob, "an' I've sailed the salt sea long enough to know."

"Land it is, thank God," said the captain earnestly, shutting up his telescope. "Get out the oars again, lads! We can't make it before dark, but the sooner we get there the better, for landing on these coral islands isn't always an easy job."

The oars were got out at once, and the men pulled with a will, but it was late at night before they drew near to the land and heard the roar of the surf on the coral reef that stood as a sentinel to guard the island.

"Captain," said Will Osten, "the wind has almost died away, yet it seems to me that the surf roars as violently as if a storm were raging."

"That surf never goes down in those seas, doctor. Even in calm weather the swell of the big ocean gathers into a huge billow and bursts in foam upon the coral islands."

"Surely, then," said Will, "it must make landing both difficult and dangerous."

"It is, sometimes, but not always," replied the captain; "for a channel of safety has been provided, as you shall see, before long. Take the boat-hook, Goff, and look out in the bows."

The man rose and stood up with the boat-hook ready to

R. M. Ballantyne

"fend off" if necessary.

A word or two here about the coral islands—those wonderful productions of the coral insect—may perhaps render the position of the boat and her subsequent proceedings more intelligible.

They are of all sizes and shapes. Some are small and low, like emeralds just rising out of the ocean, with a few cocoa-nut palms waving their tufted heads above the sandy soil. Others are many miles in extent, covered with large forest trees and rich vegetation. Some are inhabited, others are the abode only of sea-fowl. In many of them the natives are naked savages of the most depraved character. In a few, where the blessed gospel of Jesus Christ has been planted, the natives are to be seen, "clothed and in their right minds." Wherever the gospel has taken root, commerce has naturally sprung up, and the evils that invariably follow in her train have in too many cases been attributed to Christianity. Poor indeed must be that man's knowledge of the influence of Christianity, who would judge of its quality or value by the fruit of its *professors*. "By their fruits ye shall know *them*," truly—*them*, but not Christianity. The world is an hospital, and life the period of convalescence. Christianity is the one grand and all-sufficient medicine. Shall we, the afflicted and jaundiced patients, still suffering from the virulence and effect of sin, condemn the medicine because it does not turn us out cured in a single day? Still, even to fruits we can appeal, mingled and confounded with crab-apples though they be.

Come, sceptic, make a trial of it. Go to the Fiji Islands; get yourself wrecked among them. Be cast into the stormy deep; buffet the waves manfully, and succeed in struggling exhausted to the shore. The savages there, if not

Christianised, will haul you out of the sea, roast you, and eat you! They do this in compliance with a humane little law which maintains that all who are shipwrecked, and cast on shore, are thus to be disposed of. Ha! you need not smile. The record of this fact may be read, in unquestionable authorities, in every public library in the kingdom. Search and see.

On the other hand, go and get cast on one of the Fiji group where Christianity holds sway, and there, despite the errors, inconsistencies, and sins of its professors and enemies, the same natives will haul you out of the sea, receive you into their houses, feed and clothe you, and send you on your way rejoicing.

There is one peculiarity which applies to most of the coral islands—each is partially surrounded by a coral reef which lies at a distance from the shore varying from less than one to two miles. Outside of this reef the sea may heave tumultuously, but the lagoon within remains calm. The great breakers may thunder on the reef, and even send their spray over, for it is little above the level of the sea, and nowhere much more than a few yards in breadth, but inside all is peaceful and motionless. In this reef there are several openings, by which a ship of the largest size may enter and find a safe, commodious harbour. It is found that these openings occur usually opposite to any part of the islands where a stream flows into the sea; and the openings have frequently a little herbage, sometimes a few cocoa-nut palms growing on either side, which form a good natural land-mark to the navigator.

Towards one of these openings the long-boat of the *Foam* was rowed with all speed. The night was dark, but there was light sufficient to enable them to see their way. As they drew near they came within the influence of the

R. M. Ballantyne

enormous breakers, which rose like long gigantic snakes and rolled in the form of perpendicular walls to the reef, where they fell with a thunderous roar in a flood of milky foam.

Here it was necessary to exercise the utmost caution in steering, for if the boat had turned broadside on to one of these monstrous waves, it would have been rolled over and over like a cask.

"Pull gently, lads," said the captain, as they began to get within the influence of the breakers. "I don't quite see my way yet. When I give the word, pull with a will till I tell ye to hold on. Your lives depend on it."

This caution was necessary, for when a boat is fairly within the grasp of what we may term a shore-going wave, the only chance of safety lies in going quite as fast as it, if not faster. Presently the captain gave the word; the men bent to their oars and away they rushed on the crest of a billow, which launched them through the opening in the reef in the midst of a turmoil of seething foam. Next moment they were rowing quietly over the calm lagoon, and approaching what appeared to be a low-lying island covered with cocoa-nut trees; but the light rendered it difficult to distinguish objects clearly. A few minutes later the boat's keel grated on the sand, and the whole party leaped on shore.

The first impulse of some of the men was to cheer, but the feelings of others were too deep for expression in this way.

"Thanks be to God!" murmured Captain Dall as he landed.

"Amen!" said Will Osten earnestly.

Some of the men shook hands, and congratulated each other on their escape from what all had expected would prove to be a terrible death.

As for Larry O'Hale, he fell on his knees, and, with characteristic enthusiasm, kissed the ground.

"My best blissin's on ye," said he with emotion. "Och, whither ye be a coral island or a granite wan no matter; good luck to the insict that made ye, is the prayer of Larry O'Hale!"

R. M. Ballantyne

CHAPTER SEVEN

HOPES, FEARS,
AND PROSPECTS ON THE CORAL ISLAND

Few conditions of life are more difficult to bear than that which is described in the proverb, "Hope deferred maketh the heart sick." Day after day, week after week passed by, and every morning the unfortunate men who had been cast on the coral island rose with revived hope to spend the day in anxiety, and to lie down in disappointment.

The island proved to be a low one, not more than four miles in length by about half a mile in breadth, on which nothing grew except a few cocoa-nut palms. These afforded the wrecked crew a scanty supply of food, which, with the provisions they had brought, enabled them to live, but the prospect of a residence on such a spot was so hopeless, that they would have left it immediately had not an accident happened which deprived them of their boat.

A few mornings after landing, several of the men rose early, and, without obtaining the captain's permission, went to fish in the lagoon, intending to surprise their comrades by bringing a supply of fresh fish. They were unsuccessful, but, supposing that their chance would be better in the open sea, they rowed through the opening in the reef. They had, however, miscalculated the size and power of the breakers that continually thundered there. The boat was heavy and unmanageable except by a strong crew. She turned broadside to the breakers, and, in a few seconds, was hurled upon the reef and dashed to pieces. The men were saved almost by a miracle. They succeeded in landing on the reef, and afterwards, with the aid of broken pieces of the wreck, swam across the lagoon to the island.

The loss was irreparable, so that they had now no hope left except in the passing of a ship or a native canoe. This latter contingency they were led to hope for by the discovery, one very clear morning, of what appeared to be the mountain tops of a cluster of islands, barely visible on the horizon. But as day after day passed without the appearance of a canoe, they came to the conclusion that these islands were not inhabited. As weeks passed by and no sail appeared, their hearts began to fail them, for the small stock of provisions was rapidly diminishing.

One morning Captain Dall ascended to the highest point on the island, where he was wont to spend the greater part of each day on the lookout. He found Will Osten there before him.

"Good-morning doctor," said the captain, with a dash of the old hearty spirit in his voice, for he was not easily depressed; "anything in sight?"

"Nothing," replied Will, with a degree of energy in his tone that caused the captain to look at him in surprise.

"Hallo, doctor, have you made a discovery, or have you made up your mind to swim off the island, that you speak

R. M. Ballantyne

and look so resolute this morning?"

"Yes, I have made a discovery. I have discovered that the provisions will not last us another week; that our vigour is not what it used to be; that a sort of apathy is stealing over us all; that the sands of life, in short, are running out while we are sitting idle here making no effort to help ourselves."

"What can we do, lad?" said the captain sadly, supposing that the youth was merely giving vent to a spirit of desperation.

"I'll tell you what we can do," said Will, rising; "we can cut down most of the trees and make a huge pile of them, which, with the broken pieces of the long-boat to kindle them, will create a blaze that will attract the attention of the people who live on yonder island—if there be any. I know the character of South Sea islanders, but it is better to live in captivity or die by the hand of savages than to perish of hunger and thirst. Come, Captain Dall, we *must* stir the men up to make a last effort. Rather than die here, I will make a raft and hoist a sail on it, and commit myself to the winds and waves. What say you? Shall we try?"

"There is something in what you say, doctor," replied the captain, pondering the subject; "at all events, no harm can come of making the attempt. I'll go speak to the men."

In pursuance of this intention he left the place of outlook accompanied by Will, and the result of their consultation with the men was, that in a few minutes Larry O'Hale and Mr Cupples set to work with all the energy in their natures to fell trees with the two axes they possessed. When they were exhausted, Will Osten and Goff relieved them, and then the captain and old Bob took the axes.

Thus the work went on all day, and in the evening a pile of logs was raised almost as large as a medium-sized cottage.

There was something hopeful in the mere act of working with a view to deliverance that raised the spirits of the men, and when the sun began to sink towards the western horizon, they sat down to their slight meal of biscuit and cocoa-nut milk with more appetite and relish than they had experienced for many days.

"I've bin thinkin'," said Larry, pausing in the midst of his supper.

"Well, wot have 'ee bin thinkin', lad?" said Muggins, wiping his mouth with the sleeve of his coat and wishing for more food—but wishing in vain, for he had finished his allowance—"you're a good deal given to thinkin', but there's not much ever comes on it, 'xcept wind in the shape o' words."

"And what's words," retorted the cook, in supreme contempt, "but the expression o' sintiment, widout which there wouldn't have bin nuthin' wotsomediver in the univarse? Sintiment is the mother of all things, as owld Father O'Dowd used to say to my grandmother whin he wanted to come the blarney over her. It was a philosopher sintimentilisin' over a tay-kittle, I'm towld, as caused the diskivery o' the steam-ingine; it was a sintimintal love o' country as indooced Saint Patrick to banish the varmin from Ireland, an' it was religious sintiment as made Noah for to build the Ark, but for which nother you nor me would have bin born to git cast upon a coral island. Sintiment is iverything, Muggins, and of that same there isn't more in your whole body than I cud shove into the small end of a baccy-pipe. But to return to the pint: I've

R. M. Ballantyne

bin thinkin' as to whether it would be best to set a light to this here little pile in the daylight or in the dark, bekase, in the wan case it's the smoke that would call attintion, an' in the other case it's the flame."

"That is true, Larry," said the captain; "I'm inclined to think it would be better seen at night, fire being more powerful than smoke."

"But they're more likely to be asleep at night, and to miss seein' it," observed Cupples, in a hollow tone.

It may be remarked in passing, that the mate's voice had become much more sepulchral and his aspect more cadaverous since his arrival on the island.

"True for ye," chimed in Larry; "an' who knows, if they did see it, but they might take it for the moon in a fog—or for a volkainy?"

"Wouldn't the best way to settle the matter be to kindle the fire just now, before it grows dark," suggested Will Osten, "so that they will have a chance of seeing the smoke, and then, when it grows dark, the fire will be getting brighter?"

"Right, doctor, you're right. Come, we'll put the light to it at once," cried the captain, rising. "Hand me the match-box, Mr Cupples; it's in the head o' the bread cask."

The whole party rose and went to the pile of timber, which was on the highest part of the islet and towered to a height of nearly twelve feet. Captain Dall applied a match to the tarry pieces of the long-boat, which had been placed at the foundation, and the flames at once leaped up and began to lick greedily round the timber, winding through the interstices and withering up the leaves. Soon a thick smoke began to ascend, for much of the timber in the pile was green, and before the sun had set a dense black cloud was rising straight up like a pillar and spreading out into the sky. As the fire gathered strength, a great tongue of flame flashed up ever and anon into the midst of the rolling cloud and rent it for a single instant; by degrees those tongues waged fierce war with the smoke. They shot through it more and more frequently, licked and twined round it—in and out—until they gained the mastery at last, and rose with a magnificent roar into the heavens. Then it was that Larry O'Hale gave vent to his excitement and admiration in an irrepressible shout, and his comrades burst into a mingled cheer and fit of laughter, as they moved actively round the blazing mass and stirred it into fiercer heat with boat-hooks and oars.

When night had closed in, the brilliancy of the bonfire was intense, and the hopes of the party rose with the flames, for they felt certain that any human beings who chanced to be within fifty miles of them could not fail to see the signal of distress.

So the greater part of the night was passed in wild excitement and energetic action. At last, exhausted yet hopeful, they left the bonfire to burn itself out and sat down to watch. During the first half-hour they gazed earnestly over the sea, and so powerfully had their hopes been raised, that they expected to see a ship or a boat approaching every minute. But ere long their hopes sank as quickly as they had been raised. They ceased to move about and talk of the prospect of speedy deliverance. The hearts of men who have been long exposed to the depressing influence of "hope deferred," and whose frames are somewhat weakened by suffering and insufficient food, are easily chilled. One after another they

R. M. Ballantyne

silently crept under the sail, which had been spread out in the form of a tent to shelter them, and with a sigh lay down to rest. Weariness and exposure soon closed their eyes in "kind Nature's sweet restorer—balmy sleep," and the coral island vanished utterly from their minds as they dreamed of home, and friends, and other days. So, starving men dream of sumptuous fare, and captives dream of freedom.

Will Osten was last to give way to the feeling of disappointment, and last to lie down under the folds of the rude tent. He was young, and strong, and sanguine. It was hard for one in whose veins the hot blood careered so vigorously to believe in the possibility of a few days reducing him to the weakness of infancy—harder still for him to realise the approach of death; yet, when he lay meditating there in the silence of the calm night, a chill crept over his frame, for his judgment told him that if a merciful God did not send deliverance, "the end" was assuredly drawing very nigh.

CHAPTER EIGHT

IN WHICH OUR HERO SUGGESTS A PLAN WHICH GETS THE PARTY OUT OF ONE DIFFICULTY BUT PLUNGES THEM INTO ANOTHER

How long Wandering Will would have lain in the midst of his slumbering comrades, indulging in gloomy reveries, it is impossible to say, for he was suddenly startled out of them by the appearance of a black object on the sea, at a considerable distance from the shore. Will's couch was near the open entrance to the tent, and from the spot where his head lay pillowed on his coat, he could see the lagoon, the opening in the reef, and the ocean beyond. He rose softly, but quickly, and went out to assure himself that his disturbed fancy had not misled him. No—there could be no doubt about it. Grey dawn was already breaking, and enabled him to see it distinctly—a dark moving speck on the sea far outside the reef. It could not be a gull or sea-bird, he felt persuaded; neither was it a ship, for his eye during the voyage had become a practised one in observing distant vessels. It might be a boat!

Full of this idea, and trembling with hope and anxiety, he returned to the tent, and gently awoke the captain.

R. M. Ballantyne

"Sh! don't speak," he whispered, laying his hand on the captain's mouth.

"I'm convinced it is a boat," continued Will, as he stood beside the now smouldering fire, while the captain gazed long and earnestly through his telescope at the object on the sea.

"You're only half-right," said the other, with unusual seriousness, as he handed the glass to his companion; "it's a canoe—a large one, I think, and apparently full of men; but we shan't be left long in doubt as to that; our fire has evidently attracted them, and now we must prepare for their reception."

"Do you then doubt their friendliness?" asked Will, returning the glass to the captain, who again examined the approaching canoe carefully.

"Whether they shall turn out to be friends or foes, doctor, depends entirely on whether they are Christians or heathens. If the missionaries have got a footing amongst 'em, we are saved; if not—I wouldn't give much for our chance of seeing Old England again."

The captain's voice dropped as he said this, and his face was overspread with an expression of profound gravity.

"Do you *really* believe in all the stories we have heard of the blood-thirstiness of these savages, and their taste for human flesh?" asked Will, with some anxiety.

"Believe them!" exclaimed the captain, with a bitter, almost ferocious laugh; "of course I do. I have *seen* them at their bloody work, lad. It's all very well for shore-goin' folk in the old country to make their jokes about 'Cold missionary on the sideboard,' and to sing of the 'King of the Cannibal Islands;' but, as sure as there is a sky over your head, and a coral island under your feet, so certainly do the South Sea savages kill, roast, and eat their enemies, and so fond are they of human flesh that, when they can't get hold of enemies, they kill and eat their slaves. Look, you can make out the canoe well enough now without the glass; she's makin' straight for the opening in the reef. The sun will be up in half an hour, and they'll arrive about the same time. Come, let us rouse the men."

Hastening down to the tent, the captain raised the curtain, and shouted hoarsely—

"Hallo, lads, turn out there—turn out. Here's a canoe in sight—look alive!"

Had a bomb-shell fallen into the midst of the sleepers, it could scarcely have produced more commotion among them. Every one sprang up violently.

"Hooroo!" shouted Larry O'Hale, "didn't I say so? Sure it's mysilf was draimin' of ould Ireland, an' the cabin in the bog wi' that purty little crature—" He stopped abruptly, and added, "Och! captain dear, what's wrong?"

"Hold you tongue, Larry, for a little, and keep your cheerin' till you have done fightin', for it's my opinion we may have something to do in that way ere long."

"Faix, it's mysilf as can enjoy a taste o' that too," said Larry, buttoning his jacket and turning up his cuffs.

By this time the canoe was approaching the passage in the reef, and the whole party hastened to the beach, where they held a hasty council of war, for it was now clear that the canoe was one of the largest size—capable of holding nearly a hundred men—and that it was quite full of naked savages. In a few words the captain explained to the men the character of the islanders, as ascertained by himself on previous voyages, and showed how hopeless would be their case if they turned out to be heathens.

"Now," said he, "we are fifteen in number, all told, with two muskets, one pistol, three or four cutlasses, and a small supply of ammunition. If these men prove to be enemies, shall we attack them, and try to take their canoe, or shall we at once lay down our arms and trust to their generosity? Peace or war, that's the question?"

Larry at once declared for war, and several of the more fiery spirits joined him, among whom was Will Osten; for the young doctor shrank with horror from the idea of being roasted and eaten!

"I vote for peace," said the mate gloomily.

"Sure, Mr Cupples," exclaimed Larry, "I wonder at that, for it's little pace ye gave us aboord the *Foam*."

"It's not possible," continued the mate—taking no notice of the cook's remark, nor of the short laugh which followed it—"it's not possible for fifteen men, armed as we are, to beat a hundred savages, well supplied with clubs and spears—as I make no doubt they are—so I think we should trust to their friendliness."

"Bah!" whispered Larry to the man next him; "he knows that he's too tough and dry for any savage in his siven sinses to ait *him*, cooked or raw, and so he hopes to escape."

"Mr Cupples is right, lads," said the captain; "we'd have no chance in a fair fight, an' though I make no doubt we should kill double our number in the scrimmage, what good would that do?"

Some of the men here seconded the captain; the others began to waver, and it was finally decided that they should at least begin with pacific advances.

When the council broke up, the sailors went down to the water's edge and awaited her arrival. As she came nearer, it became apparent that she was a war-canoe fill with warriors. Steadily and swiftly she advanced to within a short distance of the shore. Then the paddlers suddenly ceased, and she was allowed to drift slowly in, while a splendid looking savage stood up in the bow with a shield on his left arm and a javelin in his right hand.

The chief, for such he evidently was, wore no clothing, except a piece of native cloth round his loins; but his whole body was elaborately tatooed with various devices; and this species of decoration, coupled with the darkness of his skin, did away very much with the appearance of nakedness. He seemed as if he had been clothed in a dark skin-tight dress. But the most conspicuous part about him was the top of his head, on which there seemed to be a large turban, which, on closer inspection, turned out to be his own hair curled and fizzed out artificially. Altogether he was an imposing and gigantic fellow.

When about fifty yards from the shore, the savages checked the canoe's progress and stood up. Now was the time for action, so, according to previous arrangement, the sailors laid their weapons down on the beach, and held up their hands, at the same time making such signs of friendship as they thought would be understood. The

R. M. Ballantyne

savages, who were quick-witted fellows, at once ran the canoe ashore, leaped out, and hastened towards the white men.

As they did so, Captain Dall put his telescope to his eye for a moment, wishing to scan closely the features of the chief. Instantly the whole band turned with a howl, and, making towards the canoe, jumped in and pushed off.

"Ha!" exclaimed the captain, with a smile, "these fellows have been fired at by Europeans before now. They evidently mistook my telescope for a musket."

The savages paused, and again faced about at a short distance from the beach, and the captain sought by every imaginable sign and gesticulation to remove the bad impression he had so innocently created. He succeeded. In a short time the natives again landed and advanced towards them. On drawing near, the chief stopped and made a short speech—which, of course, none of the white men understood. To this Captain Dall replied in a short speech—which, of course, none of the natives understood. Both parties looked very amiably, however, at each other, and by degrees drew closer together, when the natives began to manifest much curiosity in reference to the costume of the sailors. Soon they became more familiar, and the truth of the proverb, that, "familiarity breeds contempt," was quickly illustrated by one of the savages seizing hold of the musket which Larry O'Hale carried. The hot blood of the Irishman instantly fired.

"Let go, ye dirty bit o' mahogany," he cried, holding the musket tight with his left hand, and clenching his right in a threatening manner.

Captain Dall, foreseeing what would be the result of a

blow, sought to create a diversion by raising his telescope to his eye. The quick-sighted savage observed the motion, let go his hold of the musket and shrank behind his comrades, who, however, did not appear disposed to screen him, for they all began to dodge behind each other until the telescope was lowered.

The temporary distraction of attention which this incident caused emboldened another savage to pounce upon the other musket, which was carried by old Bob. He wrenched it out of the sailor's hand and bounded away with a shout, swinging it over his head. Unfortunately his fingers touched the trigger and the piece exploded, knocking down the man who held it, and sending the ball close past the chief's ear.

Instantly there followed a loud yell, clubs were brandished, cutlasses gleamed, and blood would certainly have been spilt had not Captain Dall suddenly seized the chief by the shoulders and rubbed noses with him. He knew this to be the mode of salutation among some of the South Sea tribes, and sought to make a last effort at conciliation. The act was reciprocated by the chief, who signed to his men to forbear.

Captain Dall now felt convinced that any undecided course of action would only render their case more desperate, so he turned to his men with a look of authority and said sternly—

"My lads, we have only one hope left to us, and that is, submission. Throw down your weapons, and put your trust in the Almighty."

The men obeyed—some with hesitation and others sullenly; they flung their cutlasses on the sand and

R. M. Ballantyne

crossed their arms on their breasts. No sooner was this done than the savages rushed upon them in overwhelming numbers, and they were instantly overpowered. Larry O'Hale and Will Osten, with some of the younger men, struggled fiercely, and knocked down several of their opponents before they were subdued, but against such overwhelming odds they had no chance. It would have been better for them had they acted on the captain's advice. Whatever is worth doing is worth doing well, and this truth is not less applicable to the act of submission than to that of resistance. The only result of their ill-timed display of valour was the tighter fastening of the cords with which the savages bound them hand and foot, and somewhat rough handling when they, with their comrades, were tossed into the bottom of the canoe.

After the sailors were secured, the natives collected the provisions that had been brought by them to the island, and stowed these also in the canoe. This occupied a considerable time, for they were so careful to avoid missing anything, that they ranged over the whole island, examining every part minutely, and leaving nothing behind that had the slightest appearance of value in their eyes. During all this time the white men were left lying in the water which had leaked into the canoe. Indeed, the valiant Larry would certainly have been drowned, but for the aid extended to him by our hero, for he chanced to have been thrown into the canoe with his face downwards near the stern, and as the water gradually settled down there from the prow, which was raised on the sand, it covered his mouth. Fortunately Will, who was near him, managed to assist the unfortunate man in his struggles so as to enable him to rest his head on the blade of a paddle!

When everything belonging to the crew of the *Foam* had been collected, the savages returned to their canoe, re-launched her, paddled out to sea, and ere long left the little coral island out of sight behind them.

R. M. Ballantyne

CHAPTER NINE

CONTAINS AN ACCOUNT OF THE DESPERATE CIRCUMSTANCES OF THE PRISONERS

Five hours passed away, during which the savages continued to paddle almost without intermission, and our hero with his friends lay fast bound in the bottom of the canoe. They suffered great pain from the swelling of their limbs and the tightening of the cords that bound them; but although Larry O'Hale, in the exasperation of his spirit, gave vent to one or two howls, accompanied by expressions that were the reverse of complimentary, no attention was paid to them until the island towards which they steered was reached.

The instant the canoe touched the sand the captives were lifted out—their hands and feet were tied together in a bunch, and, each being slung on a stout pole as one might sling a bundle, they were carried up to a native village on the margin of a wood. On the way, Wandering Will could see that the beach swarmed with natives—a fact, however, of which his ears had already assured him, for the air was filled with yells of delight as the captives were successively lifted out of the canoe. He also observed that the island appeared to be a large one, for he got a glimpse of a huge mountain rising over the tree tops. Neither he nor any of his comrades, however, had time to make many observations, for they were hurried up the beach and into the village, where they were thrown down under a rudely built hut which was covered with broad leaves.

Here the cords that fastened them were unloosed; but if this for a moment raised the hope that they were about to be set free, they were quickly undeceived by the savages, who rebound their hands behind them. Our hero, Captain Dall, Mr Cupples, Larry O'Hale, and Muggins, were then fastened with cords of cocoa-nut fibre to the several posts of the hut in such a manner that they could stand up or lie down at pleasure. George Goff, old Bob, and the others were led away. Seeing that they were about to be separated, Captain Dall suddenly called out, "Farewell, lads," in a tone so sad, that Goff looked back at him in surprise, but his captors forced him away before he could reply.

"You think we won't see them again?" said Osten, when they were left alone.

"I think not. From what I know of those savages, I fear they have taken our comrades away to be sacrificed, and that our own time will soon come."

Something between a groan and a growl escaped from O'Hale when this was said.

"Cudn't we break thim ropes, and run amuck amongst the murtherin' blackguards," he exclaimed, seizing the rope that bound him with his teeth and endeavouring to tear it—an effort which it is needless to say was futile, and nearly cost him a tooth.

"It's of no use, Larry," said the captain; "we can't help

ourselves. If the Lord don't help us, we're dead men."

Although Will Osten was much depressed, not to say alarmed, by what he heard, he could not help wondering why the captain had so suddenly lost his buoyant spirit. At the time when a slow death by starvation had stared him in the face, he had not only retained his own heartiness of spirit, but had kept up wonderfully the spirits of his companions. Now, however—when, as Will thought, they had the chance of escaping by stratagem or by force from their captors, or, at the worst, of selling their lives dearly—his spirit seemed to have utterly forsaken him. Yet the captain was only despondent—not despairing. He had seen the deeds of savages in former years, and knew that with them there was seldom a long period between the resolve to kill and the accomplishment of the crime. He feared for the lives of his shipmates, and would have given his right hand at that moment to have been free to aid them, but the attempts of himself and his comrades to break their bonds were fruitless, so, after making one or two desperate efforts, they sat down doggedly to await their fate.

It might have been a curious study to have noted the different spirit in which these unfortunate men submitted to their unavoidable doom on that occasion. The captain sat down on a log of wood that chanced to be near him, folded his hands quietly on his knees, allowed his head to sink forward on his chest, and remained for a long time quite motionless. Will Osten, on the other hand, stood up at first, and, leaning his head on his arm against the wall of the hut, appeared to be lost in reverie. Doubtless he was thinking of home; perhaps reproaching himself for the manner and spirit in which he had quitted it—as many a poor wanderer has done before when too late! He quickly changed his thoughts, however, and, with them, his position: sat down and got up frequently, frowned, clenched his hands, shook his head, stamped his foot, bit his lips, and altogether betrayed a spirit ill at ease. Mr Cupples, whose soul had from the moment of their capture given way to the deepest possible dejection, lay down, and, resting his elbow on the floor and his head on his hand, gazed at his comrades with a look so dreadfully dolorous that, despite their anxiety, they could hardly suppress a smile. As for Muggins and O'Hale, the former, being a phlegmatic man and a courageous, sat down with his back against the wall, his hands thrust into his pockets, and a quid in his cheek, and shook his head slowly from side to side, while he remarked that every one had to die once, an' when the time came no one couldn't escape and that was all about it! Poor Larry O'Hale could not thus calm his mercurial spirit. He twisted his hard features into every possible contortion, apostrophised his luck, and his grandmother, and ould Ireland in the most pathetic manner, bewailed his fate, and used improper language in reference to savages in general, and those of the South Seas in particular, while, at intervals, he leaped up and tried to tear his bonds asunder.

Thus several hours were spent. Evening approached, and darkness set in; still no one came near the prisoners. During this period, however, they heard the continual shouting and singing of the savages, and sometimes caught a glimpse of them through crevices between the logs of which the hut was built. It was not possible for them to ascertain what they were about, however, until night set in, when several large fires were lighted, and then it could be seen that they were feasting and dancing. Suddenly, in the midst of the din, an appalling shriek was heard. It was quickly succeeded by another and another. Then the yells of the revellers increased in fury, and presently a procession of them was observed approaching

R. M. Ballantyne

the hut, headed by four men bearing a sort of stage on their shoulders.

The shrieks had struck like a death-chill to the hearts of the prisoners. No one spoke, but each had recognised familiar tones in the terrible cries. For the first time some of them began to realise the fact that they were really in the hands of murderers, and that the bloody work had actually begun. Great drops of sweat rolled down the face of Muggins as he gazed in horror through one of the crevices, and his broad chest heaved convulsively as he exclaimed, "God be merciful to us, it's George Goff!" This was too true. On the stage, carried by four natives, sat the unfortunate seaman. It required no second glance to tell that his spirit had fled, and that nothing but a corpse sat swaying there, supported by means of a pole, in a sitting posture. The cannibals were conveying it to their temple, there to cut it up and prepare it for that dreadful feast which is regarded as inexpressibly repulsive by all the human race except these islanders of the South Seas, who, incredible though it may appear, absolutely relish human flesh as a dainty morsel.

At sight of this, poor Will Osten, who had never quite believed in such terrible things, sank down on his knees with a deep groan, and, for the first time in his life, perhaps, prayed *earnestly*.

O'Hale's spirit blazed up in ungovernable fury. Like a wild beast, he tore and wrenched at the rope which bound him, and then, finding his efforts unavailing, he flung himself on the ground, while deep sobs burst at intervals from his oppressed heart.

A few minutes elapsed; then there was a rush of footsteps without, accompanied by fierce yells and the waving of torches. The prisoners leaped up, feeling almost instinctively that there hour had come. A moment later and the hut was filled with natives. All were naked, with the exception of a small piece of cloth round their loins. They were tatooed, however, and painted nearly from head to foot.

The prisoners were instantly seized and overpowered, and preparations were being rapidly made to carry them away, when a shout was heard outside, and a remarkably tall, powerful, and thickly painted savage sprang in. He pushed the natives violently aside, and gave some stern orders to those who held the prisoners. The immediate result was, that the latter were released and allowed to rise, although their hands were still bound behind them. Meanwhile the tall savage, standing beside them, harangued his comrades with great energy of tone and action.

While this was going on, Larry O'Hale whispered excitedly to his companions—

"Howld on, lads, a bit. Sure I've burst the ropes at last. The moment I git howld o' that blackguard's knife I'll cut yer lashin's. Stand by for a rush."

As Larry spoke, the tall savage drew the knife referred to from his girdle, and, glancing over his shoulder, said in English—

"Keep quiet, lads. I'll do my best to save 'ee; but if you offer to fight, you're dead men all in five minutes."

Amazement, if no other feeling had operated, would have rendered the prisoners perfectly quiet after that. They waited in deep anxiety and wonder, while the tall savage continued his harangue, at the conclusion of which his hearers uttered an expressive grunt or growl, as if of assent, and then they all filed out of the hut, leaving the prisoners alone with their deliverer.

CHAPTER TEN

OUR HERO AND HIS COMRADES IN DISTRESS BECOME SAVAGE WARRIORS FOR THE NONCE

"Friend," said Captain Dall, taking the hand of the tall savage in his and speaking with some emotion, "you have been sent as our deliverer, I know, but how a South Sea islander should happen to befriend us, and how you should come to speak English as well as ye do, is more than I can understand."

"Onderstand!" exclaimed Larry; "it's past belaif. It baits cock-fightin' intirely."

A grim smile crossed the painted face of the savage, as he said somewhat hurriedly:—

"I'm no more a South Sea islander than you are, lads, but this is not the time for explanations. It's enough for you to know, in the meantime, that I'm an Englishman, and will befriend you if you agree to obey me."

"Obey ye!" cried Larry with enthusiasm, "blissin's on yer painted mug, it's warship ye we will, av ye only git us out o' this scrape."

R. M. Ballantyne

"That's so," said Muggins, nodding his head emphatically, while Mr Cupples, in tones of the most awful solemnity, and with a look that cannot be described, vowed eternal friendship.

"Well, then," said the tall man, "we have no time to waste, for you are in a greater fix just now than ye think for. About myself it's enough to know that I'm a runaway sailor; that I made my way among these fellers here by offering to join 'em and fight for 'em, and that I won their respect at first by knocking down, in fair stand-up fight, all the biggest men o' the tribe. I don't think they would have spared me even after that, but I curried favour with the chief and married one of his daughters. Now I'm a great man among them. I didn't hear of your having been brought here till half an hour ago, havin' bin away with a war party in canoes. I returned just too late to save your comrades."

"What! are they all dead?" asked Will Osten.

"Ay, all, and if you don't follow them it will only be by attending to what I tell you. My name is Buchanan, but the savages can only manage to make Bukawanga out o' that. The word means fire, and ain't a bad one after all!"

The man smiled grimly as he said this, and then resumed, more rapidly and sternly than before:—

"You have but one chance, and that is to join us. I have come to the village with the news that a neighbouring tribe is about to attack us. If you agree to help us to fight, I may manage to save you; if not your case is hopeless. There is no time for consideration. Ay or no, that's the word."

"Sure I'll jine ye, Mr Bukkie Whangy," said Larry O'Hale, "wid all the pleasure in life. It's always for fightin' I am, at laist whin—"

"I don't like to shed human blood," said Captain Dall, interrupting, "where I've no quarrel."

"Then your own must be shed," said Bukawanga firmly.

"There's no help for it, captain," said Will Osten. "'Tis better to fight for these men than to be murdered by them. What say you, Mr Cupples?"

"War," replied the mate emphatically.

"Ditto," said Muggins, nodding his head and buttoning his jacket.

"Then strip, and we'll paint you right off," said Bukawanga; "look alive, now!"

He fastened the torch which he held in his hand to a beam of the hut, and cut the bonds of the prisoners; then, going to the door, he summoned two men, who came in with a basket made of leaves, in which were several cocoa-nut shells filled with red, white, and black earth, or paint.

"What!" exclaimed Will Osten, "must we fight without clothing?"

"An' wid painted skins?" said Larry.

"Yes, unless you would be a special mark for the enemy," replied Bukawanga; "but you have no chance if you don't become in every way like one of us."

R. M. Ballantyne

Seeing that the man was in earnest, they were fain to submit. After removing their clothes, the natives began diligently to paint them from head to foot, laying on the colours so thickly, and in such bold effective strokes, that ere long all appearance of nudity was removed. Man is a strange being. Even in the midst of the most solemn scenes he cannot resist giving way at times to bursts of mirth. Philosophy may fail to account for it, and propriety may shudder at it, but the fact is undeniable. With death hovering, they knew not how near, over them, and the memory of the fearful things they had just witnessed strong upon them, they were compelled, now and then, to smile and even to laugh aloud, as the process of painting went on. There was some variety in the adornment of each, but let that of Larry O'Hale serve as an example. First of all his legs were rubbed all over with white earth, and his body with yellow. Then, down each lower limb, behind, a palm-tree was drawn in red—the roots beginning at his heels, and the branches above spreading out on his calves. Various fanciful devices were drawn on his breast and arms, and some striking circles on his back. Last of all, one-half of his face was painted red, and the other half black, with a stripe of white extending from the root of his hair down to the point of his nose. It is needless to say that during the process the enthusiastic Irishman commented freely on the work, and offered many pieces of advice to the operator. Indeed, his tendency to improve upon existing customs had well-nigh put an end to the friendly relations which now subsisted between the white men and the natives, for he took a fancy to have a red stripe down each of his legs. Either the native did not understand him, or would not agree to the proposal, whereupon Larry took the brush and continued the work himself. At this the savage indignantly seized him by the arm and pinched him so violently that he lost temper, and, thrusting the red brush into the native's face, hurled him to the ground. There was a yell and a rush at once, and it is probable that blood would have been shed had not Bukawanga interposed.

When the painting was completed, their protector led the white men (now no longer white!) to the hut of the chief. Bukawanga was received somewhat coldly at first. The chief, a large, fine-looking old man, named Thackombau, with an enormous head of frizzled hair, looked askance at the newcomers, and was evidently disposed to be unfriendly. Observing this, and that the warriors around him scowled on them in a peculiarly savage manner, most of the prisoners felt that their lives hung, as it were, upon a thread. The aspect of things changed, however, when their friend stood up and addressed the assembly.

Bukawanga had not yet said a word about the cause of his sudden return from the war expedition. It was, therefore, with much concern that the chief and his men learned that a neighbouring and powerful tribe, with which they had always been at enmity, were actually on the way to attack them; and when Bukawanga talked of the needful preparations for defence, and, pointing to the prisoners, said that they were his countrymen, able to fight well, and willing to help them, there was a perceptible improvement in the looks of the party. Finally, Thackombau condescended to rub noses with them all, and they were ordered off to another hut to have supper. This latter arrangement was brought about by their deliverer, who knew that if they remained to sup with the natives they would be shocked, and, perhaps, roused to some act of desperate violence, by the horrible sight of portions of the bodies of their poor comrades, which, he knew, were to be eaten that night. He therefore sought to divert their thoughts from the subject by sitting down and relating many anecdotes connected with his own adventurous history, while they partook of a meal of which they stood much in need.

The dishes, although new to them, were by no means unpalatable. They consisted of baked pig and yams served on banana leaves, and soup in cocoa-nut shells. Also a dish made of taro-tops, and filled with a creamy preparation of cocoa-nut done in an oven. Bread-fruits were also served, and these tasted so like the crumb of wheaten loaf, that it was difficult to believe them to be the fruit of a tree. For drink they had the juice of the young cocoa—a liquid which resembles lemonade, and of which each nut contains about a tumblerful. There was also offered to them a beverage named ava, which is intoxicating in its nature, and very disgusting in its preparation. This, however, Bukawanga advised them not to touch.

"Now, Mr Bukkie Whangy," said Larry, after having appeased his appetite, "if I may make so bowld as to ax— how came ye here?"

"The story is short enough and sad enough," replied his new friend. "The fact is, I came here in a sandal-wood trader's ship; I was so disgusted with the captain and crew that I ran away from them when they touched at this island for water. 'Tis eight years ago now, and I have bin here ever since. I have regretted the step that I took, for the devilry that goes on here is ten times worse than I ever saw aboard ship. However, it's too late for regret now."

"Ah! *too late*," murmured Will Osten, and his thoughts leaped back to England.

"The worst of it is," continued the runaway sailor, "that I have no chance of gettin' away, for the cruelty of sailors to the natives of this island has rendered them desperate, and they murder every white man they can get hold of. Indeed there would have been no chance for you but for the breaking out of war, and the fact that they are somewhat short of fightin' men just now. Not long after I landed on the island, an American whaler sent her boats ashore for water. They quarrelled, somehow, with the natives, who drove them into their boats with tremendous hooting and yells and some hard blows, although no blood was spilt. Well, what did the scoundrels do but pulled aboard their ship, brought their big guns to bear on the people, and fired on several villages—killing and wounding a good many of 'em, women and children among the rest. That's the way these fellows set the natives against white men. It was all I could do to prevent them from knocking out my brains after the thing happened."

While Bukawanga was speaking, a great commotion was heard outside.

"They're gettin' ready for action," he said, springing up. "Now, lads, follow me. I'll get you weapons, and, hark-'ee," he added, with a somewhat peculiar smile, "I heerd some of 'ee say ye don't want to spill blood where ye have no quarrel. Well, there's no occasion to do so. Only act in self-defence, and that'll do well enough; d'ye understand?"

The man gave vent to a short chuckle as he said this, and then, leading his countrymen from the hut, conducted them towards a temple, near to which a large band of warriors was busily engaged in making preparations for the approaching fight.

CHAPTER ELEVEN

A FIGHT, WHICH RESULTS IN A MISTAKE AND A HASTY FLIGHT

The horrors of war are neither agreeable to write about nor to reflect upon. However much, therefore, it may disappoint those readers whose minds delight to wallow in the abominations of human cruelty, we will refrain from entering into the full particulars of the sanguinary fight that ensued just after the arrival of Wandering Will and his friends in the island. It is sufficient to say that many lives were lost. Of course the loss of life bore no proportion to that which occurs in civilised warfare. One roar from the throats of our terrific engines of destruction will sometimes send more souls into eternity in one moment than all the fierce fury of a hundred savages can accomplish in an hour. But what the savage lacks in power he more than makes up for in cruelty and brutality. During the few days in which the fight raged, the sights that met the eyes of the white men, and the appalling sounds that filled their ears, turned their hearts sick, and induced a longing desire to escape.

The war was carried on chiefly in the way of bush fighting. Our sailors found this mode of warfare convenient, for it enabled them to act very much as spectators. Passing over the details of the brief campaign, we touch only on those points which affected the subsequent movements of the whites.

Bukawanga, who virtually acted the part of commander-in-chief, although all the chiefs considered themselves above him, moved about actively at all times to make sure that the village was properly guarded at every point. While thus employed he had, on one occasion, to pass through a piece of scrub, or thick bush, in which he heard the shriek of a woman. Turning aside he came to an opening where a man was endeavouring to kill a little boy, whose mother was doing her best to defend him. He evidently wished to kill the child and to spare the woman, but she stooped over the child and warded off the blows with her arms so cleverly, that it was still uninjured, although the poor mother was bleeding profusely from many wounds. Bukawanga instantly rushed to the rescue, and raised his club to deal the savage a deadly blow. Unobserved by him, however, another savage had been attracted to the spot, and, seeing what was about to happen, he ran up behind Bukawanga and felled him with a blow of his club. During the scuffle the woman snatched up her boy and escaped. The two savages then began to dispute as to which had the best right to cut off the head of their fallen foe and carry it away in triumph. Both of them were much fatigued with fighting, so they sat down on the back of the prostrate seaman to conduct the discussion more comfortably. The point was still undecided when Bukawanga recovered consciousness, felt the heavy pressure on his back and loins, and heard part of the interesting dialogue!

It chanced, at this point, that Will Osten and Larry O'Hale, who, from natural affinity or some other cause, always kept together, came to the spot and peeped

R. M. Ballantyne

through the bushes. Seeing two men sitting on the body of a third and engaged in an animated dispute, they did not see cause to interfere, but remained for a few minutes almost amused spectators of the scene, being utterly ignorant, of course, as to the purport of their dispute. Suddenly, to their great surprise, they beheld the two men leap into the air; the supposed dead body sprang up, and, before either savage could use his weapons, each received a strong British fist between his eyes and measured his length on the sward, while the conqueror sprang over them into the bush and disappeared.

"Man alive!" exclaimed Larry, "if it isn't Bukkie Whangy himself! Och, the murtherin' daimons!"

With that Larry leaped over the bushes flourishing his club and yelling like a very savage. But Will Osten was before him. Both savages had risen immediately after being knocked down, and now faced their new enemies. They were no match for them. Being expert in all athletic exercises, young Osten found no difficulty in felling the first of the men, while Larry disposed of the other with equal celerity. The Irishman's blood had fired at the thought of the narrow escape of his deliverer, and, still whirling his club round his head, he looked about eagerly as if desirous of finding another foe on whom to expend his fury. At that moment he caught sight of a pair of savage eyes gleaming at him from the bushes.

"Hah! ye dirty polecat," he cried, throwing his club at the eyes with all his force.

Never was there a worse aim or a better shot! The club flew high into the air and would have fallen some fifty yards or more wide of the mark, had it not touched the limb of a tree in passing. It glanced obliquely down, and, striking the owner of the eyes between the shoulders felled him to the earth.

Larry sprang upon him with a yell of triumph, but the yell was changed into a howl of consternation when he made the discovery that he had knocked down, if not killed, one of the principal chiefs of the village! To say that poor O'Hale wrung his hands, and wished bad luck to fightin' in general, and to himself in particular, gives but a feeble idea of the distress of his mind at this untoward event.

"D'ye think I've kilt him intirely, doctor dear?" he asked of Will Osten, who was on his knees beside the fallen chief examining his hurt.

"No, not quite. See, he breathes a little. Come, Larry, the moment he shows symptoms of reviving we must bolt. Of course he knows who knocked him down, and will never forgive us."

"That's true, O murther!" exclaimed Larry, with a mingled look of contrition and anxiety.

"Depend upon it they'll kill us all," continued Osten.

"And bake an' ait us," groaned Larry.

"Come," said Will, rising hastily as the stunned chief began to move, "we'll go search for our comrades."

They hurried away, but not before the chief had risen on one elbow and shaken his clenched fist at them, besides displaying a terrible double row of teeth, through which he hissed an unintelligible malediction.

They soon found their comrades, and related what had

R. M. Ballantyne

occurred. A hurried council of war was held on the spot, and it was resolved that, as a return to the village would ensure their destruction, the only chance of life which remained to them was to take to the mountains. Indeed, so urgent was the necessity for flight, that they started off at once, naked though they were, and covered with blood, paint, and dust, as well as being destitute of provisions.

All that night they travelled without halt, and penetrated into the wildest fastnesses of the mountains of the interior. Bukawanga had already told them, during intervals in the fight when they had met and eaten their hasty meals together, that the island was a large, well wooded, and fruitful one—nearly thirty miles in diameter; and that the highest mountain in the centre was an active volcano. There were several tribes of natives on it, all of whom were usually at war with each other, but these tribes dwelt chiefly on the coast, leaving the interior uninhabited. The fugitives, therefore, agreed that they should endeavour to find a retreat amongst some of the most secluded and inaccessible heights, and there hide themselves until a ship should chance to anchor off the coast, or some other mode of escape present itself.

The difficulties of the way were greater than had been anticipated. There was no path; the rocks, cliffs, and gullies were precipitous; and the underwood was thick and tangled, insomuch that Mr Cupples sat down once or twice and begged to be left where he was, saying that he would take his chance of being caught, and could feed quite well on cocoa-nuts! This, however, was not listened to. Poor Cupples was dragged along, half by persuasion and half by force. Sailors, as a class, are not celebrated for pedestrian powers, and Cupples was a singularly bad specimen of his class. Muggins, although pretty well knocked up before morning, held on manfully without a murmur. The captain, too, albeit a heavy man, and fat, and addicted to panting and profuse perspiration, declared that he was game for anything, and would never be guilty of saying "die" as long as there was "a shot in the locker." As for Larry O'Hale, he was a man of iron mould, one of those giants who seem to be incapable of being worn out or crushed by any amount of physical exertion. So far was he from being exhausted, that he threatened to carry Mr Cupples if he should again talk of falling behind. We need scarcely say that Wandering Will was quite equal to the occasion. Besides being a powerful fellow for his age, he was lithe, active, and hopeful, and, having been accustomed to hill-climbing from boyhood, could have left the whole party behind with ease.

Grey dawn found the fugitives far up the sides of the mountains—fairly lost, as Muggins said, in a waste howlin' wilderness. It was sunrise when they reached the top of a high cliff that commanded a magnificent view of land and sea.

"A good place this for us," said the captain, wiping his forehead as he sat down on a piece of rock. "The pass up to it is narrow; two or three stout fellows could hold it against an army of savages."

"Av there was only a cave now for to live in," said Larry, looking round him.

"Wot's that?" exclaimed Muggins, pointing to a hole in the perpendicular cliff a short distance above the spot where they stood.—"Ain't *that* a cave?"

Will Osten clambered up and disappeared in the hole. Soon after he re-appeared with the gratifying intelligence that it *was* a cave, and a capital dry one; whereupon they all ascended, with some difficulty, and took possession of their new home.

CHAPTER TWELVE

SHOWS HOW SOUTH SEA MISSIONARIES DO THEIR WORK, AND THAT IF THE WHITES CAN SURPRISE THE NATIVES THE LATTER CAN SOMETIMES ASTONISH THE WHITES!

For three months did Wandering Will and his friends remain concealed in the mountains. Of course they were pursued and diligently sought for by the natives, and undoubtedly they would have been discovered had the search been continued for any length of time, but to their great surprise, after the first week of their flight, the search was apparently given up. At all events, from that period they saw nothing more of the natives, and gradually became more fearless in venturing to ramble from the cave in search of food. They puzzled over the matter greatly, for, to say the least of it, there appeared to be something mysterious in the total indifference so suddenly manifested towards them by the savages; but although many were the guesses made, they were very far from hitting on the real cause.

During this period they subsisted on the numerous fruits and vegetables which grew wild in great abundance on the island, and spent their days in gathering them and hunting wild pigs and snaring birds. As Larry was wont to

R. M. Ballantyne

observe with great satisfaction, and, usually, with his mouth full of victuals—

"Sure it's the hoith o' livin' we have— what with cocky-nuts, an' taros an' bananas, an' young pigs for the killin', an' ginger-beer for the drinkin', an' penny loaves growin' on the trees for nothin', wid no end o' birds, an' pots ready bilin', night an' day, to cook 'em in—och! it would be hiven intirely but for the dirty savages, bad luck to 'em!"

There was more truth in Larry's remark than may be apparent at first sight. Vegetation was not only prolific and beautiful everywhere, but exceedingly fruitful. The bread-fruit tree in particular supplied them with more than they required of a substance that was nearly as palatable and nutritious as bread. Captain Dall fortunately knew the method of cooking it in an oven, for the uncooked fruit is not eatable. The milk of the young cocoa-nuts was what the facetious Irishman referred to under the name of ginger-beer; but his remark about boiling pots was literally correct. The summit of that mountainous island was, as we have already said, an active volcano, from which sulphurous fumes were constantly issuing— sometimes gently, and occasionally with violence.

Several of the springs in the neighbourhood were hot—a few being almost at the boiling point, so that it was absolutely possible to boil the wild pigs and birds which they succeeded in capturing, without the use of a fire! Strange to say, they also found springs of clear *cold* water not far from the hot springs.

There is a species of thin tough bark round the upper part of the stem of the cocoa-nut palm—a sort of natural cloth—which is much used by the South Sea islanders. Of this they fashioned some rude but useful garments.

"It seems curious, doesn't it," said Will Osten to Captain Dall, one day, referring to these things and the beauty of the island, "that the Almighty should make such a terrestrial paradise as this, and leave it to be used, or rather abused, by such devils in human shape?"

"I'm not sure," answered the captain slowly, "that we are right in saying that *He* has left it to be so abused. I'm afraid that it is *we* who are to blame in the matter."

"How so?" exclaimed Will, in surprise.

"You believe the Bible to be the Word of God, don't you?" said Captain Dall somewhat abruptly, "and that its tendency is to improve men?"

"Of *course* I do; how can you ask such a question?"

"Did you ever," continued the captain pointedly, "hear of a text that says something about going and teaching all nations, and have, you ever given anything to send missionaries with the Bible to these islands?"

"I—I can't say I ever have," replied Will, with a smile and a slight blush.

"No more have I, lad," said the captain, smiting his knee emphatically; "the thought has only entered my head for the first time, but I *do* think that it is *we* who leave islands such as this to be abused by the human devils you speak of, and who, moreover, are not a whit worse—nay, not so bad—as many *civilised* human devils, who, in times not long past, and under the cloak of religion, have torn men and tender women limb from limb, and bound them at the stake, and tortured them on the rack, in order to make them swallow a false creed."

R. M. Ballantyne

This was the commencement of one of the numerous discussions on religion, philosophy, and politics, with which the echoes of that cavern were frequently awakened after the somewhat fatiguing labours of each day's chase were over, for a true Briton is the same everywhere. He is a reasoning (if you will, an argumentative) animal, and our little band of fugitives in those mountain fastnesses was no exception to the rule.

Meanwhile, two events occurred at the native village which require notice. Their occurrence was not observed by our friends in hiding, because the summit of the mountain completely shut out their view in that direction, and they never wandered far from their place of retreat.

The first event was very sad, and is soon told. One morning a schooner anchored off the village, and a party of armed seamen landed, the leader of whom, through the medium of an interpreter, had an interview with the chief. He wished to be permitted to cut sandal-wood, and an agreement was entered into. After a considerable quantity had been cut and sent on board, the chief wanted payment. This was refused on some trivial ground. The savages remonstrated. The white men threatened, and the result was that the latter were driven into their boats. They pulled off to their vessel, loaded a large brass gun that occupied the centre of the schooner's deck, and sent a shower of cannister shot among the savages, killing and wounding not only many of the men, but some of the women and children who chanced to be on the skirt of the wood. They then set sail, and, as they coasted along, fired into several villages, the people of which had nothing to do with their quarrel.

Only a week after this event another little schooner anchored off the village. It was a missionary ship, sent by the London Missionary Society to spread the good news of salvation through Christ among the people. Some time before, a native teacher—one who, on another island, had embraced Christianity, and been carefully instructed in its leading truths—had been sent to this island, and was well received; but, war having broken out, the chief had compelled him to leave. A second attempt was now being made, and this time an English missionary with his wife and daughter were about to trust themselves in the hands of the savages.

They could not have arrived at a worse time. The islanders, still smarting under a sense of the wrong and cruelty so recently done them, rushed upon the little boat of the schooner, brandishing clubs and spears, the instant it touched the land, and it was with the utmost difficulty that the missionary prevailed on them to stay their hands and give him a hearing. He soon explained the object of his visit, and, by distributing a few presents, so far mollified the people that he was allowed to land, but it was plain that they regarded him with distrust. The tide was turned in the missionary's favour, however, by the runaway sailor, Buchanan, or Bukawanga. That worthy happened at the time to be recovering slowly from the effects of the wound he had received in the fight, which had so nearly proved to be his last. On hearing of the arrival of strangers he feared that the savages would kill them out of revenge, and hastened, weak and ill though he was, to meet, and, if possible, protect them. His efforts were successful. He managed to convince the natives that among Christians there were two classes—those who merely called themselves by the name, and those who really did their best to practise Christianity; that the sandal-wood traders probably did not even pretend to the name, but that those who had just arrived would soon give proof that they were of a very different spirit. The result

R. M. Ballantyne

of this explanation was, that the chiefs agreed to receive the missionary, who accordingly landed with his family, and with all that was necessary for the establishment of a mission.

Those who have not read of missionary enterprise in the South Seas can form no conception of the difficulties that missionaries have to contend with, and the dangers to which they are exposed on the one hand, and, on the other, the rapidity with which success is sometimes vouchsafed to them. In some instances, they have passed years in the midst of idolatry and bloody rites, the mere recital of which causes one to shudder, while their lives have hung on the caprice of a volatile chief; at other times God has so signally blessed their efforts that a whole tribe has adopted Christianity in the course of a few weeks. Misunderstand us not, reader. We do not say that they all became true Christians; nevertheless it is a glorious fact that such changes have occurred; that idolatry has been given up and Christianity embraced within that short period, and that the end has been the civilisation of the people; doubtless, also, the salvation of some immortal souls.

In about two months after their arrival a marvellous change had taken place in the village.

The natives, like very children, came with delight to be taught the use of the white man's tools, and to assist in clearing land and building a cottage. When this was finished, a small church was begun. It was this busy occupation that caused the savages to forget, for a time, the very existence of Wandering Will and his friends; and if Bukawanga thought of them, it was to conclude that they had taken refuge with one of the tribes on the other side of the island.

That which seemed to amuse and delight the natives most in the new arrivals was the clothing which was distributed among them. They proved very untractable, however, in the matter of putting it on. One man insisted on putting the body of a dress which had been meant for his wife on his own nether limbs—thrusting his great feet through the sleeves, and thereby splitting them to the shoulder. Another tied a tippet round his waist, and a woman was found strutting about in a pair of fisherman's boots, and a straw bonnet with the back to the front!

One of the chiefs thus absurdly arrayed was the means of letting the fugitive white men have an idea that something strange had occurred at the village. This man had appropriated a scarlet flannel petticoat which had been presented to his mother, and, putting it on with the waist-band tied round his neck, sallied forth to hunt in the mountains. He was suddenly met by Larry O'Hale and Will Osten.

"Musha! 'tis a ow-rangy-tang!" cried the Irishman.

His companion burst into a fit of loud laughter. The terrified native turned to flee, but Larry darted after him, tripped up his heels, and held him down.

"Kape quiet, won't ye?" he said, giving the struggling man a severe punch on the chest.

The savage thought it best to obey. Being allowed to get on his legs he was blindfolded, and then, with Will grasping him on one side, and the Irishman on the other, he was led up to the mountain-cave, and introduced to the family circle there, just as they were about to sit down to their mid-day meal.

CHAPTER THIRTEEN

REMARKABLE CHANGES FOR THE BETTER

It will not surprise the reader to be told that the savage with the red flannel petticoat tied round his neck was received with shouts of laughter by the inmates of the cave, and that his costume filled them with mingled feelings of astonishment and curiosity. The information obtained from him by signs did not enlighten them much, but it was sufficient to convince them that something unusual had occurred at the native village, and to induce Will Osten to act in accordance with his favourite motto.

"I tell you what, comrades," said he, after a few minutes' deliberation, "I have made up my mind to go back to the village with this red-coated gentleman, and see whether they are all decked out in the same fashion. To tell the truth, I have been thinking for some time back that we have been living here to no purpose—"

"Only hear that, now," said Larry O'Hale, interrupting; "haven't we bin livin' like fightin' cocks, an' gettin' as fat as pigs? Why, Mr Cupples hisself begins to throw a shadow on the ground whin the sun's pretty strong; an' as for Muggins there—"

"You let Muggins alone," growled the seaman; "if we *are* fatterer, p'raps it'll only be for the good o' the niggers when they come to eat us."

"Well, well," said Will; "at all events we shall never escape from this place by remaining here—('True for ye,' said Larry)—therefore I shall go to the village, as I have said. If they receive me, well and good; I will return to you. If not—why, that's the end of me, and you'll have to look out for yourselves."

As usual an energetic discussion followed this announcement. The captain said it was madness, Mr Cupples shook his head and groaned, Muggins thought that they should all go together and take their chance, and Larry protested that he would sooner be eaten alive than allow his comrade to go without him; but in time Will Osten convinced them all that his plan was best.

What would be the good of the whole of them being killed together, he said—better that the risk should fall on one, and that the rest should have a chance of escape. Besides, he was the best runner of the party, and, if he should manage to wriggle out of the clutches of the savages, would be quite able to outrun them and regain the cave. At length the youth's arguments and determination prevailed, and in the afternoon he set off accompanied by his sable friend in female attire.

On nearing the village, the first thing that greeted the eyes of our hero was a savage clothed in a yellow cotton vest and a blue jacket, both of which were much too small for him; he also had the leg of a chair hung round his neck by way of ornament.

This turned out to be the principal chief of the village,

R. M. Ballantyne

Thackombau, and a very proud man he obviously was on that occasion. To refrain from smiling, and embrace this fellow by rubbing noses with him, was no easy matter, but Will Osten did it nevertheless. While they were endeavouring to converse by signs, Will was suddenly bereft of speech and motion by the unexpected appearance of a white man—a gentleman clothed in sombre costume—on whose arm leaned a pleasant-faced lady! The gentleman smiled on observing the young man's gaze of astonishment, and advancing, held out his hand.

Will Osten grasped and shook it, but still remained speechless.

"Doubtless you are one of the party who escaped into the hills lately?" said the gentleman.

"Indeed I am, sir," replied Will, finding words at last, and bowing to the lady; "but from what star have *you* dropt? for, when I left the village, there were none but savages in it!"

"I dropt from the *Star of Hope*," answered the gentleman, laughing. "You have hit the mark, young sir, nearer than you think, for that is the name of the vessel that brought me here. I am a missionary; my name is Westwood; and I am thankful to say I have been successful in making a good commencement on this island. This is my wife— allow me to introduce you—and if you will come with me to my cottage—"

"Cottage!" exclaimed Will.

"Ay, 'tis a good and pretty one, too, notwithstanding the short time we took to build it. The islanders are smart fellows when they have a mind to labour, and it is wonderful what an amount can be done when the Lord prospers the work. These good fellows," added the missionary, casting a glance at the two natives, "who, as you see, are somewhat confused in their ideas about dress, have already done me much service in the building of the church—"

"Church!" echoed Will.

Again the missionary laughed, and, offering his arm to his wife, turned towards the village, saying—

"Come, Mr Osten—you see I know your name, having heard of you from your friend Buchanan—come, I will show you what we have been about while you were absent; but first—tell me—how fares it with your comrades?"

Will Osten at once entered into a full account of the doings of himself and his friends, and had just concluded, when he was once more rendered speechless by the sight of the missionary's cottage. It was almost the realisation of the waking dream which had captivated him so much on the evening when the storm arose that proved fatal to the *Foam*. He was still gazing at it in silent admiration, listening to an enthusiastic account of the zeal and kindness of the natives who helped to build it, when a young girl, apparently bordering on seventeen or eighteen years of age, with nut-brown curls, rosy cheeks, and hazel eyes, sprang out and hastened to meet them.

"Oh, father," she exclaimed, while the colour of her face came and went fitfully, "I'm so glad you have come! The natives have been so—so—"

"Not rude to you, Flora, surely?" interrupted the missionary.

R. M. Ballantyne

"No, not exactly rude, but, but—"

Flora could not explain! The fact turned out to be that, never having seen any woman so wonderfully and bewitchingly beautiful before, the natives had crowded uninvited into the cottage, and there, seated on their hams round the walls, quietly gazed at her to their hearts' content—utterly ignorant of the fact that they were violating the rules of polite society!

Will Osten, to his disgrace be it said, violated the same rules in much the same way, for he continued to gaze at Flora in rapt admiration until Mr Westwood turned to introduce her to him.

That same evening Bukawanga, accompanied by Thackombau, went to the mountain-cave, and, having explained to its occupants the altered state of things at the village, brought them down to the mission-house where they took up their abode.

It need scarcely be said that they were hospitably received. Mr Westwood had not met with countrymen for many months, and the mere sight of white faces and the sound of English voices were pleasant to him. He entertained them with innumerable anecdotes of his experiences and adventures as a missionary, and on the following morning took them out to see the church, which had just been begun.

"Already," said Mr Westwood, as they were about to set forth after breakfast, "my wife and Flora have got up a class of women and girls, to whom they teach needle-work, and we have a large attendance of natives at our meetings on the Sabbath. A school also has been started, which is managed by a native teacher who came with me from the island of Raratonga, and most of the boys in the village attend it."

"But it does seem to me, sir," said Captain Dall, as they sauntered along, "that needle-work and book-learning can be of no use to such people."

"Not of much just now, captain, but these are only means to a great end. Already, you see, they are beginning to be clothed—fantastically enough at present, no doubt—and I hope ere long to see them in their right mind, through the blessed influence of the Bible. Look there," he added, pointing to an open space in the forest, where the four walls of a large wooden building were beginning to rise; "there is evidence of what the gospel of Jesus Christ can do. The labourers at that building are, many of them, bitter enemies to each other. Only yesterday we succeeded in getting some of the men of the neighbouring village to come and help us. After much persuasion they agreed, but they work with their weapons in their hands, as you see."

This was indeed the case. The men who had formerly been enemies were seen assisting to build the same church. They took care, however, to work as far from each other as possible, and were evidently distrustful, for clubs and spears were either carried in their hands, or placed within reach, while they laboured.

Fortunately, however, they restrained their passions at that time, and it is due to them to add that before that church was finished their differences were made up, and they, with all the others, ultimately completed the work in perfect harmony, without thinking it necessary to bring their clubs or spears with them.

R. M. Ballantyne

The reader must not suppose that all missionary efforts in the South Seas have been as quickly successful as this one. The records of that interesting region tell a very different tale; nevertheless there are many islands in which the prejudices of the natives were overcome almost at the commencement, and where heathen practices seemed to melt away at once before the light of the glorious gospel.

During two months, Wandering Will and the wrecked seamen remained here assisting the missionary in his building and other operations. Then an event occurred which sent them once more afloat, and broke the spell of their happy and busy life among the islanders.

CHAPTER FOURTEEN

CONTAINS MORE THAN ONE SURPRISE, AND TOUCHES ON "LOVE'S YOUNG DREAM"

One quiet and beautiful Sabbath morning, the inhabitants of the South Sea Island village wended their way to the House of God which they had so recently erected. Among them were Will Osten and his friends, with the clergyman's wife and daughter.

Poor Wandering Will was very unhappy. The sunshine was bright, the natives were blithe, and the birds were joyous, but our hero was despondent! The fact was that he had fallen head and ears in love with Flora Westwood, and he felt that he might as well have fallen in love with the moon—as far as any chance of getting married to her was concerned. Will was therefore very miserable, and, like all ardent and very youthful lovers, he hugged his misery to his bosom—rather enjoyed it, in fact, than otherwise. In short, if truth must be told, he took pleasure in being miserable *for her sake*! When he allowed himself to take romantic views of the subject, and thought of the heights of bliss that *might* be attained, he was, so to speak, miserably happy. When he looked the stern realities in the face, he was miserably sad.

R. M. Ballantyne

That Sabbath morning poor Will felt more impressed than ever with the hopelessness of his case, as he walked slowly and silently to church beside the modest Flora and her mother. He also became impressed with the ridiculousness of his position, and determined to "overcome his weakness." He therefore looked at Flora with the intention of cutting a joke of some sort, but, suddenly recollecting that it was Sunday, he checked himself. Then he thought of getting into a serious talk, and was about to begin, when his eye happened to fall on Thackombau, who, in honour of the day, had got himself up with unusual care, having covered his shoulders with a cotton jacket, his loins with a lady's shawl, and his head with a white nightcap—his dark tatooed legs forming a curious and striking contrast to the whole.

Before Will could think of another mode of opening the conversation, they had arrived at the church, and here, in front of the open door, there lay the most singular contribution that ever was offered to the cause of Christianity. Many dozens of church-door plates rolled into one enormous trencher would have been insufficient to contain it, for it was given not in money (of course) but in kind. There were a number of lengths of hollow bamboo containing cocoa-nut oil, various fine mats and pieces of native cloth, and sundry articles of an ornamental character, besides a large supply of fruits and vegetables, with four or five baked pigs, cold and ready for table! The entire pile was several feet in diameter and height, and was a freewill offering of the natives to the church—the beginning of a liberality which was destined in future years to continue and extend—a species of liberality which is by no means uncommon among the South Sea Islanders, for there are some of those who were savage idolators not many years ago who now give annually and largely to the support of the missions with which their churches are connected.

Larry O'Hale had just made a remark in reference to "the plate" which was not conducive to the gravity of his companions, when the echoes of the mountains were awakened by a cannon-shot, and a large ship was seen to round the point of land that stretched out to the westward of the island. Instantly the natives poured out of the church, rushed down to the shore, launched their canoes and paddled over the lagoon to meet the vessel, which, running before a stiff breeze, soon entered the natural gateway in the reef. The congregation having dispersed thus unceremoniously, the clergyman and his friends were compelled to postpone service for a time.

The ship which had created such a sensation in the village, was also the means of causing great disturbance in sundry breasts, as shall be seen. She had called for water. Being in a hurry, her captain had resolved not to waste time by conciliating the natives, but, rather, to frighten them away by a cannonade of blank cartridge, land a strong party to procure water while they were panic-stricken, and then up anchor and away. His surprise was great, therefore, when the natives came fearlessly off to him (for he had been warned to beware of them), and he was about to give them a warm reception, when he caught a glimpse of the small spire of the new church, which at once explained the cause of the change.

With rollicking good humour—for he was a strong healthy man with a sleeping conscience—Captain Blathers, on landing, swaggered up to the clergyman and shook him heartily and gratefully by the hand, exclaiming, with a characteristic oath, that he had not much opinion of religion in his own country, but he was bound to say it was "a first-rate institootion in the South Seas."

Mr Westwood rebuked the oath and attempted to correct the erroneous opinion, but Captain Blathers laughed, and said he knew nothing about these matters, and had no time for anything but getting fresh water just then. He added that he had "a batch of noosepapers, which he'd send ashore for the use of all and sundry."

Accordingly, off he went about his business, and left the clergyman and natives to return to church, which they all did without delay.

That night the missionary went on board the ship to see the captain and preach to the crew. While he was thus engaged, our friends, Captain Dall, Mr Cupples, O'Hale, Muggins, and Wandering Will, in a retired part of the forest, held an earnest conversation as to whether they should avail themselves of the arrival of the ship to quit the island. Captain Dall had already spoken with Captain Blathers, who said he was quite willing to let them work their passage to England.

"Now, you see, comrades," said Captain Dall, thrusting his right fist into his left palm, "the only trouble is, that he's not goin' direct home—got to visit the coast of South America and San Francisco first, an' that will make it a long voyage."

"But, sure," said Larry, "it won't be so long as waitin' here till next year for the missionary schooner, and then goin' a viage among the islands before gettin' a chance of boording a homeward-bound ship?"

"That's so," said Muggins, with a nod of approval. "I says go, ov coorse."

Mr Cupples also signified that this was his opinion.

"And what says the doctor?" asked Captain Dall, turning to Will Osten with an inquiring look.

"Eh? well, ah!" exclaimed Will, who had been in a reverie, "I—I don't exactly see my way to—that is—if we only could find out if she is—is to remain here *always*, or hopes some day to return to England—"

Poor Will stopped in sudden confusion and blushed, but as it was very dark that did not matter much.

"What *does* the man mean?" exclaimed Captain Dall. "How *can* she remain here always when she's to be off at daybreak—?"

"True, true," interrupted Will hurriedly, not sorry to find that his reference to Flora was supposed to be to the ship. "The fact is, I was thinking of other matters—of *course* I agree with you. It's too good an opportunity to be missed, so, good-night, for I've enough to do to get ready for such an abrupt departure."

Saying this, he started up and strode rapidly away.

"Halloo!" shouted Larry after him; "don't be late—be on the baich at daybreak. Arrah he's gone mad intirely."

"Ravin'," said Muggins, with a shake of his head as he turned the quid in his cheek.

Meanwhile Wandering Will rushed he knew not whither, but a natural impulse led him, in the most natural way, to the quiet bay, which he knew to be Flora's favourite walk on moonlight nights! The poor youth's brain was whirling with conflicting emotions. As he reached the bay, the moon, strange to say, broke forth in great splendour, and

R. M. Ballantyne

revealed—what!—could it be?—yes, the graceful figure of Flora! "Never venture," thought Will, "never—"

In another moment he was by her side; he seized her hand; she started, suppressed a scream, and tried to free her hand, but Will held it fast. "Forgive me, Flora, dearest girl," he said in impassioned tones, "I would not dare to act thus, but at daybreak I leave this island, perhaps for ever! yet I *cannot* go without telling you that I love you to distraction, that—that—oh! say tell me—"

At that moment he observed that Flora blushed, smiled in a peculiar manner, and, instead of looking in his face, glanced over his shoulder, as if at some object behind him. Turning quickly round, he beheld Thackombau, still decked out in his Sunday clothes, gazing at them in open-mouthed amazement.

Almost mad with rage, Will Osten rushed at him. The astonished savage fled to the woods, Will followed, and in a few minutes lost himself! How he passed that night he never could tell; all that he could be sure of was that he had wandered about in distraction, and emerged upon the shore about daybreak. His appointment suddenly recurring to him, he ran swiftly in the direction of the village. As he drew near he observed a boat pushing off from the shore.

"Howld on!" shouted a well-known voice; "sure it's him-self after all."

"Come along, young sir, you're late, and had well-nigh lost your passage," growled Captain Blathers.

Will jumped into the boat and in a few minutes found himself on board the *Rover*, which, by the time he reached it, was under weigh and making for the opening in the reef.

Another hour, and the island was a mere speck on the horizon. Gradually it faded from view; and the good ship, bending over to the freshening breeze, bounded lightly away over the billows of the mighty sea.

THE END

R. M. Ballantyne

Other books by this author

Black Ivory

Red Rooney

The Coral Island

The Golden Dream

The Hot Swamp

The Island Queen

The Red Eric

Fast in the Ice

Chasing The Sun

The Battle and the Breeze

The Lively Poll

Choose from Thousands of 1stWorldLibrary Classics By

A. M. Barnard
Ada Leverson
Adolphus William Ward
Aesop
Agatha Christie
Alexander Aaronsohn
Alexander Kielland
Alexandre Dumas
Alfred Gatty
Alfred Ollivant
Alice Duer Miller
Alice Turner Curtis
Alice Dunbar
Allen Chapman
Alleyne Ireland
Ambrose Bierce
Amelia E. Barr
Amory H. Bradford
Andrew Lang
Andrew McFarland Davis
Andy Adams
Angela Brazil
Anna Alice Chapin
Anna Sewell
Annie Besant
Annie Hamilton Donnell
Annie Payson Call
Annie Roe Carr
Annonaymous
Anton Chekhov
Archibald Lee Fletcher
Arnold Bennett
Arthur C. Benson
Arthur Conan Doyle
Arthur M. Winfield
Arthur Ransome
Arthur Schnitzler
Arthur Train
Atticus
B.H. Baden-Powell
B. M. Bower
B. C. Chatterjee
Baroness Emmuska Orczy
Baroness Orczy
Basil King
Bayard Taylor
Ben Macomber
Bertha Muzzy Bower
Bjornstjerne Bjornson

Booth Tarkington
Boyd Cable
Bram Stoker
C. Collodi
C. E. Orr
C. M. Ingleby
Carolyn Wells
Catherine Parr Traill
Charles A. Eastman
Charles Amory Beach
Charles Dickens
Charles Dudley Warner
Charles Farrar Browne
Charles Ives
Charles Kingsley
Charles Klein
Charles Hanson Towne
Charles Lathrop Pack
Charles Romyn Dake
Charles Whibley
Charles Willing Beale
Charlotte M. Braeme
Charlotte M. Yonge
Charlotte Perkins Stetson
Clair W. Hayes
Clarence Day Jr.
Clarence E. Mulford
Clemence Housman
Confucius
Coningsby Dawson
Cornelis DeWitt Wilcox
Cyril Burleigh
D. H. Lawrence
Daniel Defoe
David Garnett
Dinah Craik
Don Carlos Janes
Donald Keyhoe
Dorothy Kilner
Dougan Clark
Douglas Fairbanks
E. Nesbit
E. P. Roe
E. Phillips Oppenheim
E. S. Brooks
Earl Barnes
Edgar Rice Burroughs
Edith Van Dyne
Edith Wharton

Edward Everett Hale
Edward J. O'Biren
Edward S. Ellis
Edwin L. Arnold
Eleanor Atkins
Eleanor Hallowell Abbott
Eliot Gregory
Elizabeth Gaskell
Elizabeth McCracken
Elizabeth Von Arnim
Ellem Key
Emerson Hough
Emilie F. Carlen
Emily Bronte
Emily Dickinson
Enid Bagnold
Enilor Macartney Lane
Erasmus W. Jones
Ernie Howard Pie
Ethel May Dell
Ethel Turner
Ethel Watts Mumford
Eugene Sue
Eugenie Foa
Eugene Wood
Eustace Hale Ball
Evelyn Everett-green
Everard Cotes
F. H. Cheley
F. J. Cross
F. Marion Crawford
Fannie E. Newberry
Federick Austin Ogg
Ferdinand Ossendowski
Fergus Hume
Florence A. Kilpatrick
Fremont B. Deering
Francis Bacon
Francis Darwin
Frances Hodgson Burnett
Frances Parkinson Keyes
Frank Gee Patchin
Frank Harris
Frank Jewett Mather
Frank L. Packard
Frank V. Webster
Frederic Stewart Isham
Frederick Trevor Hill
Frederick Winslow Taylor

Friedrich Kerst
Friedrich Nietzsche
Fyodor Dostoyevsky
G.A. Henty
G.K. Chesterton
Gabrielle E. Jackson
Garrett P. Serviss
Gaston Leroux
George A. Warren
George Ade
Geroge Bernard Shaw
George Cary Eggleston
George Durston
George Ebers
George Eliot
George Gissing
George MacDonald
George Meredith
George Orwell
George Sylvester Viereck
George Tucker
George W. Cable
George Wharton James
Gertrude Atherton
Gordon Casserly
Grace E. King
Grace Gallatin
Grace Greenwood
Grant Allen
Guillermo A. Sherwell
Gulielma Zollinger
Gustav Flaubert
H. A. Cody
H. B. Irving
H. C. Bailey
H. G. Wells
H. H. Munro
H. Irving Hancock
H. R. Naylor
H. Rider Haggard
H. W. C. Davis
Haldeman Julius
Hall Caine
Hamilton Wright Mabie
Hans Christian Andersen
Harold Avery
Harold McGrath
Harriet Beecher Stowe
Harry Castlemon
Harry Coghill
Harry Houidini

Hayden Carruth
Helent Hunt Jackson
Helen Nicolay
Hendrik Conscience
Hendy David Thoreau
Henri Barbusse
Henrik Ibsen
Henry Adams
Henry Ford
Henry Frost
Henry James
Henry Jones Ford
Henry Seton Merriman
Henry W Longfellow
Herbert A. Giles
Herbert Carter
Herbert N. Casson
Herman Hesse
Hildegard G. Frey
Homer
Honore De Balzac
Horace B. Day
Horace Walpole
Horatio Alger Jr.
Howard Pyle
Howard R. Garis
Hugh Lofting
Hugh Walpole
Humphry Ward
Ian Maclaren
Inez Haynes Gillmore
Irving Bacheller
Isabel Cecilia Williams
Isabel Hornibrook
Israel Abrahams
Ivan Turgenev
J. G.Austin
J. Henri Fabre
J. M. Barrie
J. M. Walsh
J. Macdonald Oxley
J. R. Miller
J. S. Fletcher
J. S. Knowles
J. Storer Clouston
J. W. Duffield
Jack London
Jacob Abbott
James Allen
James Andrews
James Baldwin

James Branch Cabell
James DeMille
James Joyce
James Lane Allen
James Lane Allen
James Oliver Curwood
James Oppenheim
James Otis
James R. Driscoll
Jane Abbott
Jane Austen
Jane L. Stewart
Janet Aldridge
Jens Peter Jacobsen
Jerome K. Jerome
Jessie Graham Flower
John Buchan
John Burroughs
John Cournos
John F. Kennedy
John Gay
John Glasworthy
John Habberton
John Joy Bell
John Kendrick Bangs
John Milton
John Philip Sousa
John Taintor Foote
Jonas Lauritz Idemil Lie
Jonathan Swift
Joseph A. Altsheler
Joseph Carey
Joseph Conrad
Joseph E. Badger Jr
Joseph Hergesheimer
Joseph Jacobs
Jules Vernes
Julian Hawthrone
Julie A Lippmann
Justin Huntly McCarthy
Kakuzo Okakura
Karle Wilson Baker
Kate Chopin
Kenneth Grahame
Kenneth McGaffey
Kate Langley Bosher
Kate Langley Bosher
Katherine Cecil Thurston
Katherine Stokes
L. A. Abbot
L. T. Meade

L. Frank Baum
Latta Griswold
Laura Dent Crane
Laura Lee Hope
Laurence Housman
Lawrence Beasley
Leo Tolstoy
Leonid Andreyev
Lewis Carroll
Lewis Sperry Chafer
Lilian Bell
Lloyd Osbourne
Louis Hughes
Louis Joseph Vance
Louis Tracy
Louisa May Alcott
Lucy Fitch Perkins
Lucy Maud Montgomery
Luther Benson
Lydia Miller Middleton
Lyndon Orr
M. Corvus
M. H. Adams
Margaret E. Sangster
Margret Howth
Margaret Vandercook
Margaret W. Hungerford
Margret Penrose
Maria Edgeworth
Maria Thompson Daviess
Mariano Azuela
Marion Polk Angellotti
Mark Overton
Mark Twain
Mary Austin
Mary Catherine Crowley
Mary Cole
Mary Hastings Bradley
Mary Roberts Rinehart
Mary Rowlandson
M. Wollstonecraft Shelley
Maud Lindsay
Max Beerbohm
Myra Kelly
Nathaniel Hawthrone
Nicolo Machiavelli
O. F. Walton
Oscar Wilde
Owen Johnson
P.G. Wodehouse
Paul and Mabel Thorne

Paul G. Tomlinson
Paul Severing
Percy Brebner
Percy Keese Fitzhugh
Peter B. Kyne
Plato
Quincy Allen
R. Derby Holmes
R. L. Stevenson
R. S. Ball
Rabindranath Tagore
Rahul Alvares
Ralph Bonehill
Ralph Henry Barbour
Ralph Victor
Ralph Waldo Emmerson
Rene Descartes
Ray Cummings
Rex Beach
Rex E. Beach
Richard Harding Davis
Richard Jefferies
Richard Le Gallienne
Robert Barr
Robert Frost
Robert Gordon Anderson
Robert L. Drake
Robert Lansing
Robert Lynd
Robert Michael Ballantyne
Robert W. Chambers
Rosa Nouchette Carey
Rudyard Kipling
Saint Augustine
Samuel B. Allison
Samuel Hopkins Adams
Sarah Bernhardt
Sarah C. Hallowell
Selma Lagerlof
Sherwood Anderson
Sigmund Freud
Standish O'Grady
Stanley Weyman
Stella Benson
Stella M. Francis
Stephen Crane
Stewart Edward White
Stijn Streuvels
Swami Abhedananda
Swami Parmananda
T. S. Ackland

T. S. Arthur
The Princess Der Ling
Thomas A. Janvier
Thomas A Kempis
Thomas Anderton
Thomas Bailey Aldrich
Thomas Bulfinch
Thomas De Quincey
Thomas Dixon
Thomas H. Huxley
Thomas Hardy
Thomas More
Thornton W. Burgess
U. S. Grant
Upton Sinclair
Valentine Williams
Various Authors
Vaughan Kester
Victor Appleton
Victor G. Durham
Victoria Cross
Virginia Woolf
Wadsworth Camp
Walter Camp
Walter Scott
Washington Irving
Wilbur Lawton
Wilkie Collins
Willa Cather
Willard F. Baker
William Dean Howells
William le Queux
W. Makepeace Thackeray
William W. Walter
William Shakespeare
Winston Churchill
Yei Theodora Ozaki
Yogi Ramacharaka
Young E. Allison
Zane Grey

www.ingramcontent.com/pod-product-compliance
Lightning Source LLC
Chambersburg PA
CBHW031845170626
46807CB00004B/1638